Happiness is a Skills

Techniques for being Happier

Jerry Dykstra
BA, MBA, CTT+, CHt

D1521380

Attention: Jerry Dykstra is not a therapist or physician. If you are struggling with negative emotions, there are many trained professionals and organizations available to help. Just do an Internet search for "Help Phone Hotlines." For emergencies, call 911.

This is not a book someone reads and puts away. Instead, it is a book one can come back to time after time, year after year.

About the Author

Jerry Dykstra, BA, MBA, CTT+, CHt, has taught Life Skills in numerous formats to a variety of diverse audiences, including high school students, people with special needs, people entering the workforce, inmates, businesspeople, and others.

This book is part of a 6-Book Life Skills Series.

The Book of Life Skills – 52 Life-Changing Lessons
Affirmations – Words for Self-Confidence
How to Make Friends – A Guide to Social Skills
How be Smarter – The Skills of Learning-to-Learn
Happiness is a Skill – Techniques for Being Happier
Visualization – Techniques for Imagination (late 2022)

They provide: (a) the Basic Concepts of Life Skills in a very simple format, (b) inspiring Words to help people build Self-Confidence, (c) coaching for Friendship and Social Skills, (d) Learning-to-Learn Skills that can help students and adults read, memorize, and learn faster, (e) strategies for being Happier, and (f) Visualization techniques to imagine one's potential.

What If...?

What if a student or young adult read all 6 of these books over time? They might not understand it all, but they could come back to them year after year. What kind of competitive edge would they have?

For more information, or to write a review, go to:

Amazon.com > Books > Jerry Dykstra

If you enjoy the book, it would be very helpful if you could write a review. That way other people can enjoy it.

Why this Book was Written

One would hope people would naturally grow up learning the basic skills of how to be Happy. In reality, many students and adults struggle as they pass through the various phases of life.

The goal of this book is to write down basic:
- Vocabulary words
- Concepts
- Strategies, and
- Techniques

... in a very simple and easy-to-read format.

If there are sections or a chapter that are either too basic or too detailed, just skip to the next section and go on.

Table of Contents

1 - WHAT ARE LIFE SKILLS?

Life Skills classes started because students were growing up without learning things often called "Common Sense." Classes included topics on how to open a bank account, buy a car, do a monthly budget, eat nutritional food, etc. Many Life Skills are very basic and easy to learn.

The Mental Skills

Over time, the classes evolved to include the <u>Mental Skills</u>, which teach how to:
- Build Self-Confidence
- Manage Emotions
- Learn Social Skills
- Set and Achieve Goals
- Improve Learning Skills
- Develop Personal Motivation
- Overcome Adversity
- Be Happy

The opportunities Life Skills provide can be summarized in the following options.

- <u>Option A</u> – If someone spends 20 years learning, they will have a reasonable understanding of the lessons of life. The problem is the next generation has to learn the same information all over again by themselves.

- <u>Option B</u> – If somebody could <u>write down</u> the basic concepts in a very simple, easy-to-understand format, that would provide opportunities for students and adults to get along with people better, accelerate their learning abilities, and achieve more of their goals.

CHAPTER 2 – WHAT IS HAPPINESS?

<u>Happiness</u> is a very important Life Skill, but not too many people have taken a course on it.

Often, people think Happiness is something that happens <u>to</u> them. When it is a nice day, they feel good. When it is dark and raining, their mood also becomes gray. If someone is rude to them, they feel bad. If they receive a compliment, they feel better. They may <u>not</u> understand how to influence their own level of personal satisfaction.

Happiness can consist of 4 Steps.
- Understanding <u>Happiness is a Skill</u>, something that can be learned.
- Developing the <u>Desire</u> to be Happier.
- Learning the <u>strategies</u> and <u>techniques</u>.
- <u>Practicing</u> the techniques over time.

Happiness means very different things to different people. What does it mean to you?

What Happens When You Are Happy?
1. When you are really happy, what do you do? You can add your own ideas.
   - Smile
   - Cheer
   - Laugh
   - Jump up and down
   - Hug somebody
   - "High Five" your friends
   -
   -
   -

2. What <u>Thoughts</u> go through your mind?

3. How do you <u>Feel</u>?

THE HAPPINESS METER

-10	-5	0	+5	+10
Very Unhappy				Very Happy

On the scale above, "<u>-10</u>" means the person is very Unhappy. A "<u>+10</u>" rating means they are *very Happy*. The "<u>0</u>" in the center is in between being Unhappy (-) and Happy (+).

The <u>Happiness Meter</u> has many applications. Taking your temperature with a thermometer lets you know if you have a fever or are healthy. A Happiness Meter rating from <u>-10 to 0</u> is like telling someone they have a fever. It could be temporary or serious.

A rating of <u>0 to +5</u> reflects a person is happy. It's wonderful when someone is in the <u>+5 to +10</u> range because they are <u>very</u> happy.

What is it like to be at a "+10?"
Have you ever watched the Super Bowl and one team scored a winning touchdown in the last few seconds of the game? How did the audience react? Were they screaming, jumping up and down, and hugging each other? That's what a "+10" is like.

Another time when people are very happy is when they have met someone new. They might start thinking about that person often during the day. As they do, they start to smile. Over time, they realize they are falling in love. Their "head is in the clouds." That also can be a "+10."

What Influences the Meter?
What are the things that influence people to have a positive score? What puts you in a positive "Mood?" Can you repeat the experience at other times when you want?

It is okay to dip below "0" occasionally, but if it happens too often, it is a suggestion to talk to a friend, parent, or counselor.

How Do You Describe Happiness?
Words not only are used to reflect our Moods, they also influence moods. If someone is using Positive words like "Motivation," "Passionate," and "Loving," they are likely moving toward a positive rating on the Happiness Meter. If someone is using Negative words like "Anger," "Fear," and "Disappointment," they are likely moving toward a negative rating. When other people use angry words toward us, we also get angry. On the other hand, inspirational words can motivate us to take action. The Lesson is,

the Words people use influence their Happiness.

Unhappy Words	Happy Words
Uncomfortable	Feeling great!
Lonely	Friendly
Hate	Love
Negative	Positive
Fearful	Hopeful
Embarrassed	Self-Confident

Angry	Loving
Ashamed	Proud
Lazy	Energetic
Discouraged	Excited
Greedy	Generous

What is a Skill?

When people hear, "Happiness is a Skill," they can sometimes be confused.

Definition: Skill – The ability to do an activity well. Having an expertise in something. Examples include playing the piano, painting a picture, or being good at a sport.

In sports, the coaches break down the activity into processes, and the athletes practice each process until they become good at it. In baseball, players learn how to hit, run, pitch, catch, and play the outfield.

Happiness also has a number of Processes that can be learned. Many are "common sense" because a lot of people already know them.

In football, teams practice all week and play only one game a week. For the Olympics, athletes will practice for years to prepare for their events.

Does "being Happy" qualify as something a person can also learn to do well, like a sport? Yes. Happiness is a Skill with Structure, Processes, and specific Techniques to learn.

HAPPINESS TECHNIQUES

Definition: Potential – Abilities that can be developed over time. The best one can be. Performing at a top level.

Life is a set of Skills
that can be taught and learned
to help people achieve more of their Potential.

There are always Options available, as we will see in the stories of Role Models, who appeared to have very little reason to have hope, but...

CHOSE to Dream anyway.

ROLE MODEL: The Greatest Teacher Ever?

At an early age, Ann Sullivan's mother died, and her father deserted the family making her an orphan. She became blind at age 5 and attended the Perkins School for the Blind in Boston.

Years later, an operation restored much of her vision. When she graduated from the school at the age of 20, a request arrived for someone to help a girl who was deaf and blind. So, she traveled to Alabama to help Helen Keller (1880-1968). As you can imagine, it was very difficult trying to teach somebody who could not see or hear. Most people would have thought it was impossible. Another problem was Ann's social skills were not very well developed, and she was socially awkward.

Over time, Ann taught Helen how to communicate with hand gestures. Then, she coached her through high school and helped her graduate from Radcliffe College. Later, Helen became an internationally known public speaker. As a result, Ann has been recognized as one of the <u>greatest teachers ever</u>.

The question is, how did she do it? How did she ever do what everyone else thought was impossible – teach a deaf and blind girl to become educated and famous? She was barely educated herself, had no family, and was 1,000 miles from Boston. *Anyone else* would have given up and done something else. One possibility might have been,

> Her desire to help someone else gave her the
> ability to keep trying.
> (Sources: Movie - *The Miracle Worker* (1962), Wikipedia.org)

<u>LESSON</u>: Here was a person who had extremely difficult struggles in her life, yet she had the <u>compassion</u> to improve someone else's life.

Good Thoughts can inspire people to achievements beyond their previous imagination.

For some, that might be a new concept. They might believe their Potential is *defined* by other People and Events <u>outside</u> their control. However, it might be that their <u>Beliefs</u> are holding them back, not their environment.

What people <u>Believe</u> often determines what they become.

Could you learn how to expand your mind with new <u>Thoughts</u>? Could you learn how to use <u>Thoughts</u> as <u>Tools</u> to bring happiness and joy to yourself and others?

We will study other Role Models who faced exceptional Adversities only to rise above them.

The Benefits of Happiness

There are Many Benefits of Happiness.
1. Self-Confidence
2. <u>Friends</u> and <u>Loved Ones</u> who provide support
3. <u>Job</u> success
4. Achieving personal <u>Goals</u>
5. Willing to <u>try</u> new things
6. Feeling good
7. Being healthy
8. The joy of helping others
9. Peace of mind
10. Self-Actualization

EXERCISE: Three Good Things About Me
In Life Skills classes, a favorite exercise is to have students come to the front of the class and tell everyone 3 good things about themself. After they say each good thing, everyone in the class cheers for them.

What are 3 good things about you?

1.

2.

3.

What Are Your Favorite Things?

Write down the Events that are most important to you. It is okay to skip any topic that doesn't interest you.

1. Trips and Vacations
    - What was your best vacation, and what did you do?

    - Where would you like to go on vacation?

2. Friends
    - Who is your best friend?

    - What do you like about them?

3. Family
    - Who are the members of your family?

    - What do you enjoy doing together?

4. Social Events/Parties - What social events do you enjoy?
    - Birthday Parties
    - Weddings
    - What is your best holiday?
    - Other Events

5. <u>Going to the beach or pool</u>
   - Do you have a special place to go swimming?

6. <u>Enjoying Food</u>
   - What is your favorite food?

   - Why do you like it?

   - What is the best snack or dessert?

   - What is a restaurant you really like?

7. <u>Learning New Knowledge</u>
   - Do you go to school?

   - What's your best subject?

   - What will you do when you graduate?

8. <u>Sporting Events</u>
   - What is your favorite sport?

   - What is your favorite team?

   - Who is the best player?

9. <u>Music – Listening, Singing, and Playing an Instrument</u>
   - What is your favorite song?

   - Do you have a favorite singer or band?

   - Can you sing or play an instrument?

10. Personal Victories
    - What personal victories have you had – awards, prizes, graduation, etc?

11. Relaxation
    - What is your preferred way to Relax?

12. Pets
    - Do you have a pet? What is its name?

    - Would you like to have a pet?

13. Movies/Books
    - What is your favorite movie?

    - Who is your favorite star?

    - Is there a favorite book you like?

14. Work
    - Do you have a job?

    - What do you like about it?

    - Do you have friends there?

15. <u>Computer Activities</u>
    - Do you have a favorite computer game?

    - What are your preferred social media websites?

16. <u>Past Memories</u>
    - What are your favorite memories?

    - Who else is with you?

17. <u>Dreams of the Future</u>
    - What Dreams do you have?

    - Do you have any specific Goals to accomplish?

18. <u>Others</u>
    - What other things make you happy?

<u>SUMMARY</u>
1. What was the best <u>Event</u> of your life (graduation, wedding, etc.)?

2. What conditions created the Event?

3. How did you <u>Feel</u> when it was happening?

EXERCISE: The Treasure Chest of the Mind

One way to enjoy your special Events is to write them down on a sheet of paper or in a Journal. What if you made a long list? That way, anytime you needed a "boost," you could start to think about your Favorite Thoughts and recall them.

Possibly, you could start to write the list down right here. That way you could start enjoying them now. Wouldn't it be nice to have a Treasure Chest of the Mind, where you can open up your Favorite Thoughts and enjoy them any time you want?

Who is Dr. Perspective?

Dr. Perspective and his Student are characters from previous books. They will be helping occasionally to emphasize certain perspectives and key points.

CHAPTER 4 - PERSPECTIVE - CHOOSING HOW WE SEE

There are many ways we can "see" Events, People, and Ourselves.

The Half Full Glass

There is the classic story about a glass of water that is 50% filled. The story is so old, it has even been said as a joke. Some people see the Glass as half full, while others see it as half empty. It is a Metaphor (teaching story) for having a Positive or Negative Attitude.

One person might be Happy because the water is *available*, while another can be angry because some of it is *missing*. The applications go way beyond 6 ounces of water. The lesson has a lot to do with people seeing what they want to see or what their mind is *programmed* to see. Here are some other examples of events people see differently.

- Two employees work next to each other in an office. One hates their job and feels they are not getting paid enough. They can't wait until the end of the day. The other person is really excited and stays late each night because they imagine their career is just starting to take off. However, both have the exact same job.
- If 2 students get a "B+" on a test, they may not see it in the same way. A struggling student might see it as a great "triumph," while the honor student might see it as a "disappointment."
- Two athletes go to the Olympics. One did not place for any medals but is so excited about just being there. It is the high point of their life. Another athlete is standing on the podium receiving a medal. However, their head is hung in humiliation because the medal was silver (2nd Place), instead of gold.

So, there are a multitude of ways people can <u>Interpret</u> events.

Many don't realize how many <u>choices</u> they have. However, with just a little education, a world of opportunities can open up.

<u>LESSON</u>: It's not always the event that makes us happy or sad. Sometimes, it is how we "see" the event that determines our emotions.

Have you thought much about
what <u>you</u> Think about?

Does it make you weaker or stronger?

Some people have their daily <u>Thoughts</u> (worry, anger, etc.) make them weaker. Others are constantly <u>inspired</u> by their Thoughts (Imagination, Dreams, Love, etc.), which makes them stronger.

Definition: <u>Perspective</u> – Being able to "see" something from a <u>Point of View</u>. Different Perspectives give us the ability to see things in different ways.

Definition: <u>Perception</u> – A picture. A point of view. The "angle" one looks from. An interpretation of an event. What is seen from a Perspective?

An example of Perspective would be top vs. bottom, front vs. back, close vs. far away, etc. Does the front of a car look like the back of a car?

<u>Dr. Perspective:</u> Most people have developed their Perspectives (ways of seeing) from their:
- Beliefs
- Habits
- Attitudes

Over time, someone can learn the skills of <u>Perception Modification</u>, which is the process of looking at Events from different Points of View and *choosing* the Perception that is most to their advantage.

<u>Student</u>: That's crazy. Someone can't just choose to see things the way they want.

<u>Dr. Perspective:</u> Of course, they do. People frequently see and hear what they <u>want</u>. Their Attitudes and Beliefs <u>Filter</u> what enters their minds. However, rather than have their Subconscious Mind randomly select how they "see," what if they could learn to choose the viewpoint that benefits them? If 2 people are having an argument, do you think they are actually listening to each other's point of view? Probably not.

<u>Student</u>: That all seems pretty complicated to me.

<u>Dr. Perspective:</u> It is very complicated. If it was easy, everybody would be doing it. Then, everyone would be very, very happy. That is not the case. However, the Potential is available. By learning some very simple concepts, a person's ability to "see" people, events, and ideas can *improve* significantly.

Four Types of Perspective

1. <u>Perspective of LOCATION</u>

What we "see" and how we <u>interpret</u> what we "see" is often determined by the location. Most people can only think from their own (1st Person) point of view.

Can you <u>imagine</u> an Event from <u>another person's</u> Perspective? Most likely, you have already done that in the past with a family member – sister, brother, or parent.

- 1st Person – "I" or "me." This is the most common viewpoint to see from.
- 2nd Person – "You." This is the other person or the one being spoken to. The terms *sympathy* and *empathy* are

used to describe what it is like to understand the feelings of others. Many people *don't* like a 1st Person who *talks too much* and dominates the conversation. They also do *not* like to be *told* what to do by someone else. So, they may have different feelings about what was said by the 1st Person.

- 3rd Person – Someone watching from a distance can have a more analytical point of view. If 2 people are arguing very emotionally, the 3rd Person, using a more distant Perspective, might think both of the arguing people are acting foolishly.
- The 10,000 Foot View – This is like looking at the event from an airplane to see the Big Picture. Often, being too close to an event might present a very distorted view because only a small portion of the event can be seen at one time.

2. The Perspective of TIME

The Perspective of Time can change significantly depending on where one is on the Timeline.

- Yesterday means the Event has already happened. Often, there is *not* much that can be changed about what has already been done.
- "NOW" means right now, or "in the Moment." That might be a very wonderful experience enjoying what is happening right now. It can also have a disadvantage for people because they are too close to the situation and get caught up in the *emotions* of the event.
- 1 Hour Later, people sometimes wish they did not say or do what they did when they were "in the moment."
- Tomorrow can often present the Consequences or Benefits that resulted from the Event from the day before.
- A month later, it could be everyone forgot about the Event completely, or the Consequences could have become more influential over time.

If a person has always viewed the world from the 1st Person (Me) point of view, understanding the 2nd Person Perspective (You), and 3rd Person Perspective (from a distance) can open opportunities for making new friends and having better relationships.

3. The Perspective of SELF-IMAGE
The way we "see" ourselves often influences how we "see" Events. Previous experiences have a great influence on what we "see" and how we "interpret" what we see.
   a. Knowledge – The information one learns from school, college, and reading books has a major impact on how we gather information. The more education someone gets, the more vocabulary words they learn, which allows them to think in more powerful ways.
   b. Experiences – Work and life experiences also have an impact upon what we "see." Parents often see an Event differently than their teenagers. A teacher may see things quite differently than a student.
   c. Upbring – Many beliefs and actions learned from childhood are carried over into adult life. Some children are taught the skills of Self-Confidence, making new friends, and trying new things. Others can be taught, by words or actions, that their opinions have little value, which can have an impact later in life.
   d. Beliefs shape what we see. Common Beliefs form the foundation blocks of personality by directing our actions without us being aware of them. For example, someone who believes they are "no good at math," will likely find math hard to learn. Someone who has been told over the years they are "very good at math" will likely find learning math much easier.

Therefore, a Self-Image determines how a person "sees" themself. Do they have a Lack of Self-Confidence that makes them feel *uneasy* when they meet new people? Would a Self-Confident person feel more *comfortable* about meeting others and looking forward to making new friends (See Ch. 13.)?

4. The Perspective of MENTAL ATTITUDE
    A Mental Attitude can be Negative or Positive and will shape the way people see events, people, and life. Our attitude actually influences how we see.

Negative or Positive Attitude

Each person can have options.
- They can go out each day acting Gloomy and be withdrawn, or they can *smile* and be Friendly to attract other people.
- Someone can be Self-Centered and Rude by insulting others, or they can show Respect to each person they meet.
- They can focus on a Bad event from long ago that can *never* be changed, or they can Forgive the person or event from the past and look *forward* to life with *anticipation*.

The Attitude Determines the Results

- When someone has a Negative Mental Attitude, their mind will look for Negative things, so they will feel Bad more of the time,
  or
- If they have a Positive Mental Attitude, their mind will look for Positive things, so they will feel *Good* more of the time.

EXERCISE: Two Personalities
Imagine you have 2 people working with you. One has a Negative Mental Attitude and complains constantly. The other has a Positive Mental Attitude with enthusiasm and a sense of humor. Which would you like to have work with you more often?

Money

Student: It is all about money. If I had a lot of money, I would be really happy.

Dr. Perspective: That is not always the case.

The problem is, there are people who appear to "have it all," but they can't appreciate it. You would think money would fix everything, but sometimes, it doesn't. Here are 2 people who had it all.

Elvis Presley (1935-1977)

Elvis was known as the "King." A lot of real kings probably wished they had what Elvis did. He had it all – fame, fortune, and fans everywhere he went. Someone once said, if Elvis wanted anything, somebody would get it for him just to get on his good side. Unfortunately, the excesses of the "good life" got the best of him. He died of a heart attack at the age of 42.

Marilyn Monroe (1926-1962)

Marilyn also had adoring fans and many people who loved her. She made about 30 films. In today's dollars, they would have grossed over $2 billion. Despite having all the things most people would love to have, she was sad and died at the age of 36. The famous baseball player, Joe DiMaggio, who was her husband, had flowers delivered to her grave for 20 years after she died.

Happiness is a Skill
that sometimes
is hard for people to do.

A Student in Class

A young Student in a Life Skills class told the other students how she was thankful for her many Blessings.

Who was the _wise_ person? Who was the _happier_ person? Was it one of the "Stars" who had everything a person could want and died before their time, or the young student in the Life Skills class?

As someone learns this _ability to see_ new Perspectives, their mind can see things they might not have imagined before.

Conscious vs. Subconscious Mind

Definition: Conscious Mind – The mind we think and talk with.

Definition: Subconscious Mind – The mind below the Conscious Mind that controls the Beliefs and Habits.

Decisions about Beliefs are often made on the Subconscious Level. A person going to an important meeting doesn't say to themself, "_Today, I think I will go with the sloppy look._" Nobody starts the day thinking, "_I feel like today would be a good day to be rude to everyone._" However, something in their past causes them to make those decisions without the Conscious Mind thinking it over.

It can be the result of years, or even decades, of mental programming that occurs daily in the Subconscious Mind. The way people Think, their Beliefs, and their Self-Image guide their actions. What would happen if those Components were raised to the Conscious level? Would we continue with the _same_ programs, or would we consider _revising_ them, if we had a choice?

As we will learn, people with what appear to be "hopeless" lives have risen _beyond_ what most people can imagine, because of the Adversity that happened to them (See Ch. 18).

A surprising phenomenon is a disproportionate number of Olympic athletes got into their sport because of some illness or injury.

Their rehabilitation got them started, and they just *kept going* until they were the best in the world.

It wasn't their <u>Talent</u> that made them Stars,
it was their <u>Desire</u> to
overcome their <u>MISFORTUNE</u> that made them Stars.

It was <u>only</u> because of the <u>misfortune</u>,
they went to the Olympics.

These concepts can totally *redefine* common Perceptions of the relationship between talent and achievement.

Everybody is presented with numerous <u>options</u> many times during their life. The challenge is to recognize the Benefits when they appear.

1. Life Skills consist of "Common Sense" topics people learn over time. When they are written down, someone can learn the information much quicker than learning them over 20 years.
2. A Skill is something someone learns to do with practice over time. Many people learn Skills in school (reading and writing) and playing sports.
3. Mental Skills are Skills about how people can learn to Think, including developing a positive Self-Image, learning Social Skills, and managing Emotions.
4. Happiness is a Skill that may be a new idea to some people. However, learning to be Happy is like learning to do math problems or practicing a musical instrument, except few people practice their happiness Skills daily.
5. The first step is determining what makes you Happy. When we study Role Models, we learn people with numerous disadvantages have risen to achieve exceptional results.
6. A Treasure Chest of the Mind is a collection of Favorite Memories that can be recalled upon in times of difficulties.
7. Perspective is a point of view we use to "see" or "interpret" Events. When we look at Events using different Perspectives, we can choose a "view" that is best for us.
8. Location, Time, Self-Image, and Mental Attitude are Perspectives we can use to "view" events in different ways.
9. One's Perspective is based upon their Beliefs, Habits, and Attitudes.
10. A Negative Mental Attitude seeks the bad things in people and life. A Positive Mental Attitude seeks to find the good things.
11. Sometimes, people with riches and fame struggle with Happiness, while someone with much less can appreciate their many blessings.

5 - MANAGING HAPPINESS

Most people are not familiar with the term "Managing Happiness." However, managing one's Happiness can be a valuable concept, that opens up many new opportunities.

The mind is very much like a computer. There is hardware (the Brain) and software (the Programs) that processes information. The computer has a Memory to save data. People who manage computers study how they work and what to do when they break down.

How do you "turn on" your Mind in the morning? First, you wake up. Do you take a shower or have a morning cup of coffee to help the process? How do the Programs (Habits) work? What Switches can you press to move from one activity to another? How do you enter information into your mind (using sight or hearing)? How do you save data in the memory and retrieve it later? Can you print (type or write down) the information? Is there some kind of virus protection to keep it healthy and running smoothly (taking vitamins)? What are the "Troubleshooting Steps" when it isn't working correctly?

Computer technicians, who manage computers, know how to do those activities. People can also learn similar skills to manage their lives.

Reactions to Events

Events are things that happen in life. When different Events happen to you, how does your mind think about them? How does the body react? What facial expressions are made? Does the heart rate change? How does the stomach react?

Below is a list of Events with some common responses people have experienced.

- An <u>old friend</u>, from long ago, calls on the phone.
    - There is instant excitement as the mind recalls fond memories of good times from years ago.
- Somebody tells a really <u>funny joke</u>.
    - The body has a physical reaction and starts laughing.
- You see a video of a returning soldier surprising his young children after being away on a foreign tour for a long time.
    - That tender moment can bring a tear to the eye.
- Somebody says, *"Who wants Pizza?"*
    - Smiles come on the faces. Mouths waters. *"I do! I do!"*
- Your favorite basketball team won a game in "March Madness," the NCAA championship.
    - Everybody starts to jump up and down while screaming with joy.
- A group of friends shout, *"Surprise! Happy <u>Birthday!</u>"*
    - The heart might skip a beat, and then joy comes.
- You just realized you <u>lost</u> your mobile phone.
    - How did you feel?
    - Then, how did you feel when you found it?
- Somebody says, *"<u>I love you.</u>"* for the first time.
    - It can be a memory that can last for a lifetime.
- You received a gift of a large sum of money.
    - A person's outlook can change very quickly.

<u>Student:</u> What does that all mean?
<u>Dr. Perspective:</u> When events like those occur, how quickly does it take for your <u>mind</u> and <u>body</u> to respond?

In <u>seconds</u>,
- Your thoughts change.
- Your body chemistry changes.
- Your Self-Talk reflects your mood.
- There is a Physical Reaction.

The <u>LESSON</u> is, outside <u>Events</u> can dramatically change our mental states and body chemistry very quickly, even instantly.

If outside Events and People can do that <u>TO</u> us, couldn't we figure out similar <u>Words</u> and <u>Actions</u> that would have a similar impact <u>FOR</u> us?

Could we learn to Manage our own emotional states?

He Chose an Option

<u>Rob Jones</u> is a Marine veteran who lost both legs in Afghanistan in 2010. He spent a long time in recovery.

Rob had every excuse to give up and accept his status as a victim. Many people would have done that. After all, what kind of future could he have? At times, it probably looked very bleak.

Instead, he decided to prove to himself he wasn't defeated. In 2017, he ran <u>31</u> marathons in <u>31</u> days to inspire other injured veterans to imagine their potential. How could somebody do that? Why did he do that? He <u>decided</u> he would be <u>BIGGER</u> than the bad event that happened to him (Source: Wikipedia.org).

The Lesson of Rob Jones

What Lesson was veteran Rob Jones teaching when he ran 31 marathons in 31 days? People are often presented with 2 options.

- <u>Choice A</u> – Let an <u>unfortunate event</u> determine their Life
  <u>or</u>
- <u>Choice B</u> – Use the unfortunate event as motivation for achieving an <u>Exceptional</u> event.

If Rob Jones' story was unique, it would not be much of a story. However, a pattern has emerged that shows many of the greatest achievements in history often occurred <u>because</u> some Tragic Event presented itself, and the injured person <u>chose</u> to <u>overcome</u> it.

What kinds of <u>Thoughts</u>
can your mind create?

How could your <u>Thoughts</u>
motivate you?

<u>Thoughts</u> are power.
<u>Words</u> are power.
<u>Self-Confidence</u> is power.
<u>Beliefs</u> are power.
<u>Dreams</u> are power.
<u>Options</u> are power.

We all have choices.

Managing Happiness is a **<u>Skill</u>**
that can be **<u>taught</u>** and **<u>learned</u>**,
while providing
great **<u>Rewards</u>**.

CHAPTER 6 - WHAT IS THE STRUCTURE?

<u>Student:</u> What does Happiness look like?

Heredity vs. Environment

There is an old debate regarding why people act the way they do relating to <u>Heredity</u> and <u>Environment</u>. Are people the way they are because they <u>Inherited</u> the genes (DNA) from their parents, or is it because of their <u>Environment</u> (how they grew up)? The answer is <u>both</u> have an impact. The thing to realize is, those events are in the <u>past</u>. So, what are the other components that can be helpful?

Self-Image

<u>Definition: Self-Image</u> – How a person "sees' themselves. How they view their past accomplishments and their future. The Self-Image is often a cause for a Negative or Positive <u>Mental Attitude</u>.

Daily Inputs

Each day, we are bombarded with <u>Events</u>, <u>People</u>, and <u>Thoughts</u> that can have an impact upon our Emotions.

Beliefs

<u>Beliefs</u> are concepts we think are true. Some people have the belief that they "can't' do things like math, artwork, or public speaking. Others have very big Beliefs about their Potential.

Many Beliefs are buried in the <u>Subconscious Mind</u>, so people often do <u>not</u> even realize their Beliefs are controlling their actions.

Habits

Another component of the Subconscious Mind is <u>Habits</u>, which are activities we do without thinking. Examples include:

- Choosing a favorite brand of soda
- Watching the same TV show each week
- Brushing your teeth after breakfast
- Checking out the same websites
- Driving the same way to work
- Locking the car after parking it
- Taking vitamins in the morning

All those Processes (Heredity, Environment, Events, People, Thoughts, Beliefs, and Habits) go into creating a person's Attitude, which often breaks down into a:
- Negative Mental Attitude – Seeing the bad things in the world.

  or
- Positive Mental Attitude – Seeing the good things in the world.

What's for Real?
There can be a significant difference between an:
- Actual Event – What really happened as seen by an impartial observer.

  or
- How the Event is seen through the Perspective of someone's Beliefs and Attitudes.

What's the Power?
There are two ways we can *influence* how we Feel about Events:
- We can change our Perspective of the Events (how we see them),

  or
- We can change the actual Processes themselves to convert unpleasant tasks into Pleasant Tasks.

Once we understand the Processes we have available, we can use the Tools to change the Processes for our benefit.

Student: So, how does all that go together?

THE STRUCTURE OF BEING HAPPY

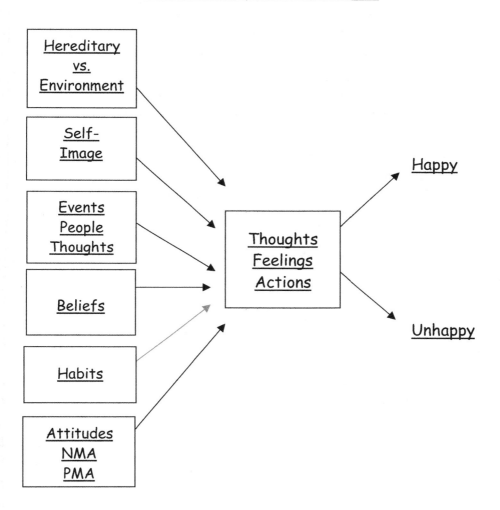

Once we can understand the Structure and Processes, the next step is to learn how to manage the different Tools.

The VERY BASIC Steps to Achieving Happiness

There are some specific things one can do to create happiness.

1. <u>Define</u> what Happiness is for you.
2. Learn how to <u>Recognize</u> your Moods and <u>Measure</u> the intensity of your Emotions.
3. <u>Identify</u> what <u>Events</u>, <u>People</u>, and <u>Thoughts</u> make you **Happy**.
   - Do the things that make you Happy <u>more</u> often.
   - Learn how to *enhance* and *amplify* those things, so you can enjoy them more.
4. <u>Identify</u> what <u>Events</u>, <u>People</u>, and <u>Thoughts</u> make you **Unhappy**.
   - Do what makes you Unhappy <u>less</u> often.
   - Learn how to change the things that make you Unhappy to make them *more enjoyable*.
5. Learn how to <u>Switch</u> from Unhappy emotions to Happy emotions.

Of course, this is a very <u>oversimplified</u> analysis. There are other modifications to this concept in <u>Ch. 10 – Motivation)</u>.

CHAPTER 7 - THE PRIMARY TOOLS

Here are <u>Seven Tools</u> used for managing one's Feelings.

1. <u>Thoughts</u>
   One strategy is to <u>reduce</u> the thinking about <u>Negative Thoughts</u> (fear and worry) and <u>increase</u> thinking about <u>Positive</u> Thoughts.

   <u>The Power of Positive Thinking</u>, written in 1952 by Norman Vincent Peale, promoted the concept that people can learn how to manage how they think. Since then, hundreds of books have been written about how to use the power of the mind.

2. <u>Self-Image</u>
   A Self-Image is a "picture" of how we see ourselves – smart, strong, weak, shy, confident, etc.

3. <u>Beliefs</u>
   When we replace untrue <u>Negative</u> Beliefs with helpful <u>Positive</u> Beliefs, we can make better decisions and grow in Potential.

4. <u>Habits</u>
   Habits are created when someone does the same thing over and over again. After a while, the Subconscious Mind takes over, so the Conscious Mind does not have to think about it anymore. An example would be, once you learn how to ride a bike, you don't have to think about how to pedal the bike anymore.

5. <u>Mental Attitude</u> – Our attitude determines how we cope with our environment. A person with a <u>Negative Mental Attitude</u> focuses on all the *bad* things in their surroundings. Someone with a <u>Positive Mental Attitude</u> has made a decision to see

more of the *good* things. You can imagine what a difference that makes.

6. <u>Primary Sensory Channels</u>
    The 3 Primary Sensory Channels include <u>Sight</u>, <u>Sound</u>, and <u>Actions</u>, which can open up new ways of thinking, communicating, and learning (See Ch. 10).

7. <u>Mental Rehearsal</u>
    Mental Rehearsal is when athletes use their Visualization Skills to practice their events in their minds. It also has many applications in the non-sports world. With some education and practice, we can learn to manage these Tools to our advantage.

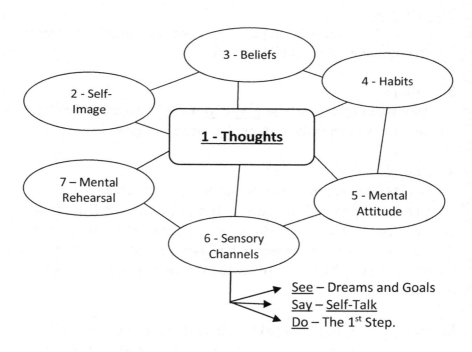

USING THE SEVEN PRIMARY TOOLS

TOOL 1 - THOUGHTS

Thoughts are pictures and ideas that come into the mind. What is the **Power** of **Thoughts**? Thoughts can...

- Make you sad.
- **Make you happy.**
- Make you cry.
- **Make you cheer.**
- Create fears that are not there.
- **Create hope when there is none.**
- Remember anger.
- **Imagine love.**
- Create worry.
- **Provide peace of mind.**
- Tell you to give up.
- **Help you to rise up.**
- Make you think you can't.
- **Inspire you to believe you CAN!**

However, our greatest power might be...

Thoughts can
help us
Change our Minds.

If Thoughts are Power,
what powerful Thoughts can we think?

TOOL 2 – SELF-IMAGE

Many people know how to create their own Negative Self-Image.

- They don't recognize the good events around them and focus on the bad events.

- They forget about their good <u>features</u> and focus on their "weaknesses."
- They recall their bad <u>memories</u> and ignore their good memories.
- They remember their <u>worries</u> and forget about their <u>dreams</u>.
- They <u>blame</u> themselves for things that were <u>not</u> in their control and <u>ignore</u> their triumphs when they occur.

When people think that way, it makes life <u>Harder</u> for them.

Understand, creating a <u>Negative</u> Self-Image takes <u>effort</u>. Your mind has to sort through all the Events of Life and <u>pick out</u> all the "bad" ones and <u>skip over</u> all the "good" ones. It takes effort to get a <u>wrong</u> "picture" of each day. It is not even logical or fair.

<u>Self-Confidence can be a Choice:</u>
- <u>Choice A – Lack of Self-Confidence</u> – Say and Believe negative things about yourself that are not true, so you don't accomplish the things you want to do,
  <u>or</u>
- <u>Choice B – Develop Self-Confidence</u> – Replace the old negative Beliefs with positive Beliefs that are true, helpful, and inspiring. <u>Recording</u> your progress and achievements daily can help you feel *more* Self-Confident.

As more and more people become aware they can <u>choose</u> to be Self-Confident, new opportunities start presenting themselves.

<u>THE SELF-IMAGE EXERCISE</u>
The <u>Self-Image Exercise</u> is like a <u>Mental Push-Up</u>. Each time you do it, you get stronger.

What are ACHIEVEMENTS you are proud of (graduation, jobs, sports victories, a hobby, etc.)?

    1.

    2.

    3.

    4.

What are your best SKILLS (sports, hobbies, making friends, a favorite class in school, musical instrument, etc.)?

    1.

    2.

    3.

    4.

What are your favorite DREAMS (new car, new job, first house, vacation, someone to love, etc.)?

    1.

    2.

    3.

    4.

Could you put this information on a 3" x 5" card to remind yourself of your Blessings during the week when things don't turn out the way you hoped? When you have negative feelings, could you read the card to help change your Mental State?

TOOL 3 - BELIEFS

<u>Beliefs</u> are Ideas, Feelings, and Events people accept (believe). They can be <u>valuable</u> or <u>harmful</u>.

- <u>Negative Beliefs</u> cause a negative impact upon a person. Some examples are, "I can't do it." "I'm not smart." "I'm not good with other people." Negative Beliefs like that often *inhibit* learning and growth. Usually, they are <u>un</u>true.

- <u>Positive Beliefs</u> *empower* a person to believe, "I CAN!" "I have the power within me." "I have a dream." These beliefs encourage people to imagine their future.

<u>Beliefs are Like Doors</u>
Sometimes, they let <u>Thoughts</u> (ideas) come in,
and sometimes,
they keep <u>Thoughts</u> (ideas) locked out.

When 2 people are presented with the <u>same</u> information, they might end up with 2 very different Perspectives. This can be because of their age, education, upbringing, job, life experiences, beliefs, or mood at the time.

Some scientists believe Habits control a major portion of our activities. We tend to eat the same food, talk to the same people, do the same job, and watch the same TV shows. It is like being on "automatic pilot."

<u>Beliefs -True or False?</u>
<u>Beliefs</u> can be:
- <u>True</u> – There is evidence showing the Belief is *true.*
- <u>False</u> – There is evidence proving the *Belief* is untrue.
- <u>Valuable</u> – It is *helpful* to the person who accepts it.
- <u>Harmful</u> – It is unhealthy for the person by preventing them from doing what they could do.

Many people have numerous <u>false</u> and <u>harmful</u> Beliefs that are the <u>basis</u> for their <u>Belief System</u>. However, the way they have "seen" life in the past does <u>not</u> mean they must have the same nonproductive Beliefs in the future.

With a little understanding, the Negative harmful Beliefs can be replaced by valuable Positive Beliefs.   See Chapters 17, 18 & 19.

TOOL 4 – HABITS

<u>Definition: Habit</u> - Doing the same thing over and over again until it finally becomes part of the Subconscious Mind. Then, the Conscious Mind does not have to be occupied by it. For example, you don't have to worry about your breathing, heart beating, or food digesting.

Habits are very powerful. When negative Habits are created, they repeatedly do things that are not good for a person. On the other hand, when one creates a *positive* Habit, it can produce good results year after year. The best way to start a Habit is by taking the First Step and repeating the process each day.

For example, good habits might include:
- Starting the day with a positive thought.
- Going for a walk to relax at the end of the day.
- Doing events now, instead of procrastinating.
- Making people smile when you meet them.
- Creating a "Priority List" at the start of each day.

TOOL 5 – MENTAL ATTITUDE

Mental Attitudes can be very different.

Negative Mental Attitude	Positive Mental Attitude
Thinks negative thoughts	Thinks positive thoughts
Says negative words	Says positive words
Focuses on weaknesses	Focuses on strengths
Blames themselves	Works on doing better

A person with a <u>Negative Mental Attitude</u> will see the world as a dark and threatening place. The Person with a <u>Positive Mental Attitude</u> will see an enthusiastic and wonderful place. However, they both live in the <u>same</u> world.

TOOL 6 – THE PRIMARY SENSORY CHANNELS

The <u>Primary Sensory Channel Model</u> includes <u>Sights</u>, <u>Sounds</u>, and <u>Actions</u> for learning, motivation, and creativity.

- <u>Visualization - Sight (See)</u> – A visual person can use their mind creatively, even when their eyes are closed.
- <u>Auditory – Sound (Say)</u> – When someone uses <u>Self-Talk</u>, they are having a conversation with themself. <u>Affirmations</u> are a special type of Self-Talk designed to program the Subconscious Mind.
- <u>Kinesthetic -Touch (Do)</u> – One of the most powerful ways to influence the subconscious mind is by taking the <u>First Step</u>. <u>Persistence</u> is a Tool for pushing on when meeting adversity.

TOOL 7 – MENTAL REHEARSAL

<u>Mental Rehearsal</u> in sports is when an athlete shuts their eyes and imagines performing their athletic event in their mind. It is a great way to practice and is very beneficial for learning. When they make a mistake, they just <u>erase</u> the image and <u>try</u> again. So, it can become a very accelerated way of learning.

MENTAL REHEARSAL EXERCISES FOR FRIENDSHIP

Just relax in a comfortable chair and imagine the following exercises. It is okay to start very slowly. Imagine what another person would look like and where you would meet. If anything goes wrong, you can just "<u>erase</u>" and <u>try again</u>.

EXERCISE: Reading People – What information can a person gather about someone else based upon their appearance, what they say, and how they say it? Select a person you know and determine what you could learn about them from the following:

Smile	Eye Contact	Attire
Posture	Handshake	Grooming
Body Langage	Attention to Detail	Voice Control
Enthusiasm Level	Sense of Humor	Interest

What kind of messages are people sending, or trying to send to others? Their body language might be saying, "*Welcome!*" "*I am important.*" "*I am a professional.*" "*I am tough.*" "*I am creative.*" "*Be my friend.*" "*I am happy.*" "*Leave me alone.*"

The First Impression is an opportunity. Many people going to a job interview do not prepare and practice meeting people. They don't know how to make a good first impression. That means, if you can understand and apply the basic principles, you will have a significant advantage when looking for a new job or making a new friend.

All these Tools are related and influence each other to determine how we Feel.

A CHOICE – WHAT DETERMINES HAPPINESS?
Which will dominate a person's Feelings?
- Outside Events and People
  or
- Their own Thoughts, Words, and Actions?

Emotions can bounce up and down during a day as a result of outside events. On the other hand, when one's Self-Confidence is built upon the blocks of Positive Beliefs and Positive Habits, we will be less dependent on the random events of the day for our happiness.

EXERCISE: Seeing through Negative and Positive Mental Attitudes

Imagine a person has 2 pairs of glasses. When they look through the "Dark Pair," everything seems dark, gloomy, and angry. When they look through the "Bright Pair," everything is *bright, sparkling,* and *cheery.* That is the difference between seeing through a Negative Mental Attitude and a Positive Mental Attitude.

Four Basic Mental States

There are the elements of <u>Pain</u> vs. <u>Pleasure</u> that dominate emotions. In addition, there are high and low energy states. Together, they create the <u>Four Basic Mental States</u>.

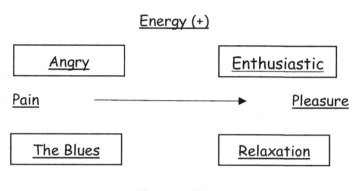

<u>Enthusiastic</u> – High Energy Pleasure
<u>Relaxation</u> – Low Energy Pleasure
<u>Angry</u> – High Energy Pain
<u>The Blues</u> – Low Energy Pain
(Source: James Loehr – <u>Mental Toughness</u> 1986)

Question
How can people learn to <u>move</u>
from the Negative Mental States to
the Positive Mental States?

Answer
The way you **Think** becomes the way you **Feel**.
The way you **Feel** becomes what you **Do**.
What you **Do** becomes what you **Think**.

Feelings are a major factor in our enjoyment of life.

47

What THOUGHTS could someone think
that will help them
feel better and be more productive?

Why Understanding Feelings is Important

If a computer does not work, the technician will say, "What is the problem?" If the person does not understand anything about computers, they might say, "I don't know. It is broken." That is not very helpful.

If a person is in an uncomfortable state, somebody might say, "What is the problem?" If the person does not understand anything about Feelings, they might say, "I don't know. I feel bad." So, it is important for people to have a working knowledge of Mental States and Feelings.

Negative Feelings can be high energy ANGRY feelings, low energy BLUE feelings, or a mixture of both. Here are some samples.

Hatred	Worry	Selfishness
Fear	Anxious	Confused
Jealous	Hopeless	Lost
Withdrawn	Scared	Lonely

These terms are good to understand because they help *define* the problems. The next step is to determine how to reduce the consequences of the negative Feeling and replace them with Positive Feelings.

Positive Feelings can be high energy ENTHUSIASTIC, low energy RELAXATION, or a combination of both.

Joyous	Surprised	Successful
Calm	Inspired	Grateful
Passionate	Loving/Loved	Peaceful
Healthy	Creative	Hopeful

If "Passionate" is not part of a person's active vocabulary, their mind likely will not have being "passionate" as an option. What is "passionate?" How does one achieve it? One of the benefits of learning new vocabulary words is, they provide people with more options to overcome negative Thoughts.

Definition: Passionate – Loving to do something. Having a strong desire to do an activity.

When a person learns that being *Passionate* is even possible, they can find something they Love to do like a new job, hobby, or sport.

Two Special Feelings

Boredom is a very powerful and common Feeling. However, rather than being caused by people or events, it is caused by the LACK of activity (people and events). People can be slightly irritated, or they can get very agitated when they become bored.

Fear is a high energy Painful Mental State that makes people ANGRY. A Fear Event can create a physical and mental response based upon a real or imagined threat.

Often, Fear is hidden. Procrastination (the Habit of putting things off) is frequently an excuse for covering up a Fear. A solution is to focus on a Dream until the Dream is more powerful than the Fear, allowing a person to move forward.

One Thought at a Time
The mind normally can only think of
One Thought at a time.

For example, most people cannot think of: (a) being at the beach on a warm summer day <u>and</u> (b) jumping out of an airplane with a parachute at the <u>same</u> time. The beach creates a very peaceful feeling, while parachuting creates a great deal of excitement. So, understanding this concept can become *very* useful. One technique is to...

Replace the <u>Negative</u> Thought
with a <u>Positive</u> Thought.

When someone thinks a Positive Thought, it can push the Negative Thought out of the mind.

What <u>Pleasant Thoughts</u> from your <u>Treasure Chest of the Mind</u> (Chapter 3) could you use to replace a Negative Thought?

A SWITCH

<u>DEFINITION</u>: <u>A SWITCH</u> – A way to use <u>Thoughts</u>, <u>Words</u>, and physical <u>Actions</u> to change a mental state. A solution for a Negative Mental State is to create a SWITCH to <u>break up</u> the Negative Mental State.

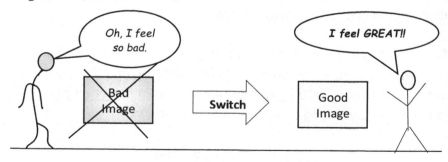

The 3 Steps of a SWITCH

1. A <u>Negative Image</u> produces Negative <u>Feelings</u>.
2. A <u>Physical Action</u> (snapping one's fingers, saying a word out loud, etc.) can help to break up the Negative Image.
3. Then, the Negative Image can be <u>replaced</u> with a <u>Positive</u> Image.

Tools for Enhancing the SWITCH include:
1. Positive <u>Images</u> from your <u>Treasure Chest of the Mind</u>
   - Beach, pool, lake
   - A vacation
   - Friend
   - Role Model

2. <u>Sounds</u>
   - <u>Self-Talk</u> – *"You can do it."*
   - <u>Affirmations</u> - *"I am completely relaxed."*
   - Words like, *"Stop." "Change" "Do it Now!"* can be used to break up the old state.

3. <u>Physical Actions</u>
   - Snap your fingers
   - Make a fist
   - Clap your hands
   - Touch 2 fingers together
   - Raise a hand in the air

Sometimes, people will pick a very *quiet* physical action, like <u>touching 2 fingers together</u> or <u>making a fist</u>, so that nobody around them will notice.

Living in "THE MOMENT"

Too often, people are doing numerous things at the same time. Someone might be watching TV, talking to a friend, and eating their favorite dessert all at once. So, they might miss out on the taste of the delicious dessert.

An alternative strategy is to *slow down* and <u>enjoy</u> the moment. That would include forgetting the past and the future for a while and just *enjoying* the experiences of the "<u>Now</u>."

Going for a walk is a simple example. It can be a wonderfully pleasurable experience. How does it feel to enjoy the first day of spring after a long winter? What is it like to feel the warmth of the sun? What is it like to breathe the refreshing air? What does "peace of mind" feel like?

There are so many pleasures in Life available
to those who are willing to *slow down* and
ENJOY them.

Working "Hard"
Working "Hard" is when people meet Adversities (bad events) and use their energy for creating BAD FEELINGS and SELF PITY. Their Self-Talk might include:

Why me?   I can't believe it!
I can't do anything right.   I always have bad luck.
This always happens to Me.   Nobody likes me.

Of course, everybody has said things like that, especially when we were younger. However, as we look at those words from the Perspective of Time, we can realize, many of those Thoughts were false. There is no reason to Catastrophize (magnify and exaggerate) them into Self-Sabotaging negative Beliefs. That is called "working hard" because it can take an unpleasant event and makes it worse (harder).

Being Reactive vs. Being Proactive
Here are two other strategies for managing negative Feelings.
- Reactive Strategy: Respond to an Event and the negative Feelings that came with it after it happens.
- Proactive Strategy: Anticipate the Negative Event and take action before it happens. Proactive can be thinking positive thoughts at designated times of the day like upon awaking, having lunch, and going to sleep.

Is it Real or Make-Believe?

When scientists do experiments, they frequently have a <u>test</u> group of people (who get the medicine) and a <u>control</u> group (who get a placebo – a fake medicine that does nothing). Nobody knows if they got the real or fake medicine. Often, the people who receive the fake medicine report feeling better because they <u>believe</u> they got the real medicine.

The concept of <u>Self-Fulfilling Prophesies</u> says, if somebody <u>believes</u> something is going to happen to them, it often <u>does</u>. Negative Beliefs ("I'm not good at math." "I could never do that." "Nobody likes me.") often become <u>true</u> because people tell themselves these things many times during the day. Then, their Subconscious Mind just <u>follows</u> the <u>instructions</u>.

What happens when a person is trying to overcome some adversity, and someone says, *"How do you feel?"* To respond to the question, they go back into their memory bank, pull up the relevant images and feelings to answer the question.

We live in a society dominated by "Feelings." However, there are other options that might also be helpful.

Five <u>Questions</u> to ask about a Negative Event.
- OPTION 1 - How do you <u>FEEL</u>?
- OPTION 2 - What do you <u>THINK</u>?
- OPTION 3 – What can you <u>SAY</u>?
- OPTION 4 – What did you <u>LEARN</u>?
- OPTION 5 – What will you <u>DO</u>?

OPTION 1 - FEEL

If someone uses <u>OPTION 1 - FEEL</u>, it focuses on their Emotions because they are in a 1st <u>Person Perspective</u>, which uses the <u>Right (Emotional) Brain</u>.

OPTION 2 - What do You THINK?

An alternative view is <u>OPTION 2</u>. What do you <u>THINK</u> about the situation? That opens up the <u>Left (Logical) Brain</u>.

Why did the event happen? Did you do something that caused it, or was it outside your control? Are there any long-term consequences, or will it be all forgotten by tomorrow? Did the Event open up any new <u>Opportunities</u>? One way to start the process is to say,

1,2,3.
What's best 4 me?

That is a type of <u>SWITCH</u> which allows the mind to "<u>Stop!</u>" Then, it can move from the <u>Right (Emotional) Brain</u> and go to the <u>Left (Logical) Brain</u>.

Just looking at an Event from the <u>Left Brain</u> can make us feel better. Why? As we look at the same event from the 3rd <u>Person Perspective</u>, we are more <u>removed</u> from the event. We can also look at it from the <u>10,000 Foot View</u> to see the <u>Big Picture</u>, which is even farther removed. In addition, using the Perspective of Time, the question might be,

Is this event actually going to have any
impact on my life in a day, week, or month from now?

OPTION 3 - What Can You SAY?

Negative Self-Talk, with an excessive amount of Self-Criticism, can create <u>Self-Pity</u>. That can cause going back to the Comfort Zone and not participating in social events. Alternative thoughts could be:

- *I am stronger than this.*
- *I am not going to let this event drag me down.*
- *I can rise above.*
- *Does this event open up any opportunities?*

OPTION 4 - What Did You LEARN?
- Were there any Lessons?
- What worked?
- What didn't work?
- Is there a better way to do it?
- Did you learn what not to do in the future?

For example, sometimes young children eat too many candies and get a stomach ache. What did they learn? They learned not to eat so many candies at one time.

When something bad happens, someone can focus on Feeling bad, or they can realize the Feelings can be managed, manipulated, and changed very quickly using another Perspective. Is there any lesson to be learned?

Negative Events often teach Lessons. A "Mistake" will seem less painful when someone realizes they just learned a valuable lesson from it.

OPTION 5 - What are you going to DO?
- Can you fix it?
- Can you do something to make up for it?
- How can you make a recovery?
- Was it a Turning Point?
- Could you apologize and make things better?

An old saying is,

Actions speak louder than words.

Definition: Turning Point - A major Life Change can happen at the Bottom of a negative Life Experience that can cause a spectacular comeback. That means the pain of a very Negative

Event can provide the <u>Motivation</u> to achieve an exceptionally positive event.

Everybody has *options* and various ways to "see" Events. Some options can be painful, and some can be *valuable*, depending upon how they <u>choose</u> to see them. A lot of it is about the amount of <u>Desire</u> the person has.

<u>Definition</u>: <u>Desire</u> - How much a person wants something. Desire can result from <u>wanting</u> a positive event or <u>fleeing</u> from a negative event.

<u>SUMMARY</u>: Feelings are one of the most important factors for our enjoyment. When a Negative Event happens, people have numerous options to <u>feel</u>, <u>think</u>, <u>say</u>, <u>learn</u>, and take <u>action</u>, which might have the potential to turn the bad event into a *Positive Event* in the long run. There are many ways to look at Events. When someone realizes their options, they can have more control of their emotions.

<u>WARNING</u>: This is a very <u>simplified</u> analysis of Feelings. If you are struggling with negative emotions, there are numerous Phone Help Lines with trained professionals ready to provide help. For an emergency, call 911.

CHAPTER 9 - MANAGING STRESS

What is Stress?

Stress wears people down physically and weakens their Self-Confidence.

Definitions for Managing Stress

- <u>Fear</u> - A reaction to <u>one</u> threatening event.
- <u>Stress</u> - A reaction to <u>numerous</u> events, some of which can be minor. One by one, each event could be handled. Together they can cause <u>distress</u>.
- <u>Stress Triggers</u> - Events that cause stress.

Managing Stress is a <u>Skill</u> that consists of a variety of <u>simple techniques</u> that are easy to learn. Many people already know what some of them are. Once a person learns the techniques, they have the <u>option</u> of using them to their advantage.

What are the Consequences of Stress?

Some medical professionals suggest 50% or more of physical illness is the result of the way people <u>Think.</u> When they have stress, their minds are occupied with so many things, they can't calm down. The result is <u>adrenaline</u> starts pumping in the body, and their mind starts saying, "*Danger! Danger! Something BAD is going to happen! Let's get ready for the battle!*"

Of course, there is <u>no battle</u> in the traditional way. There is no lion, enemy warrior, or cliff anybody is about to fall off. Instead, it is a whole collection of little, annoying things that can take their toll.

When somebody is highly stressed, they *don't* <u>Sleep</u> well, which makes the next day even more difficult. So, it can become a cycle from one day to the next.

In addition, Stress is hard on <u>Relationships</u> and family members. Have you ever been in a group, and everybody was having a good time. Then, somebody showed up who was very upset and feeling bad. That can ruin a good time for everybody else. Stress not only impacts the person with the stress, it also affects those <u>around</u> them.

THE STRESS METER

Stress can be analyzed to identify different levels? By "reading" a person's <u>Stress</u> Level, someone can imagine a built-in <u>Alarm</u> <u>System</u> to warn when they start getting to the unhealthy Levels.

Let's start at the Bottom with **Level "1"** and read upward.

<u>Level 5 – Overwhelmed – Lost of Control</u>
<u>Level 4 – Highly Emotional State</u> - Constantly worrying and verbalizing one's emotions by <u>talking out loud</u>.
<u>Level 3 – Body Reaction</u> – Physical changes start to impact the body. The person is talking to themself <u>in their mind</u>.
<u>Level 2 – Mental Discomfort Level (Higher)</u>
Level 1 – Annoyance Level (Lowest)

Once someone can *visualize* and *imagine* the <u>5 Levels</u>, they can recognize their rising level of tenseness. For example, *"I can feel my body reacting. That means I'm at <u>Level 3</u>."* Another way to measure one's level is noticing the Self-Talk. If they are talking to themself <u>in their mind</u>, they are at <u>level 3</u>. If they are talking <u>out loud</u> in a self-critical way, they are at <u>Level 4</u>.

Then, they have the <u>choice</u> of applying a <u>Solution</u> to lower the stress level. They might say, *"It is time to take a break and relax for a while."* That is not so hard to do.

THE STEPS FOR MANAGING STRESS
1. Understanding Stress
2. Recognizing Stress Triggers
3. Modifying Beliefs About Stress
4. Learning Relaxation Techniques
5. Stress-Reducing Activities
   - End Multitasking
   - Hobbies
   - Exercise

STEP 1 – UNDERSTANDING STRESS
Many people have stressful lives and don't realize stress is something they can learn to manage. Being Stressed is Hard (Painful). It is Hard on the body and mind. However, there are many techniques designed to manage it. So, the first step is to realize Stress is something that can be Managed. The Stress Meter helps to identify the Stress Level, suggesting when action can be taken.

Reactive Strategies – Actions that neutralize high-stress levels after they occur. For example, if someone feels stressed, taking a break and having a cup of tea is a way to *refresh* oneself.

Proactive Strategies - Being Proactive means creating strategies to manage the various Triggers BEFORE they happen. What activities could be done to prevent daily stress?

STEP 2 – RECOGNIZING STRESS TRIGGERS
Stress Triggers are Events, People, and Thoughts that create stress. Instead of a single event, there are numerous layers of events that create it. Once someone has identified a Stress Trigger, they can develop both Proactive and Reactive strategies.

STRESS TRIGGERS

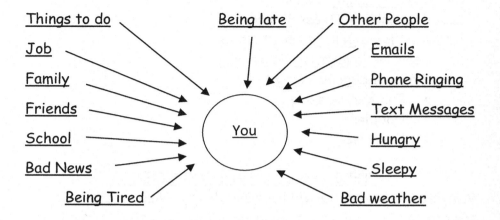

Common Stress Triggers

1. <u>Physical Triggers</u> – When these events occur, people are more vulnerable to stress.
   - A <u>Lack of Sleep</u> can be both a *Trigger* and a *Result* of stress.
   - <u>Hunger</u> – If somebody is hungry, their energy level will drop.
   - <u>Multitasking</u> – Trying to do numerous things at the same time means poor performance.
   - <u>Procrastination</u> – Putting things to do off day after day. The more things that keep being put off, the more things there are to worry about.
   - <u>Poor Diet</u> – Eating too many unhealthy foods like candy, coffee, and high-energy drinks can cause a person to be tense.
   - Being <u>Overwhelmed/Exhausted</u> is a result of too many events happening at once. <u>Taking a *deep breath*</u> can add more oxygen to the blood system, which helps relaxation. Also, try doing 1 thing at a time.

2. <u>People Triggers</u> – Other people have various problems that can create stressful environments.
   - <u>Family Members</u> – Parents, children, and spouses
   - <u>Work/School</u> – Bosses, coworkers, and other students can create demands, deadlines, and conflicts.
   - <u>Peers</u> – Hostility, meanness, selfishness, and envy by others can make someone feel bad.
   - <u>Events</u> – Work overloads, setbacks, excessive noise, complaining, phone ringing, etc.

   Family members and friends can also be the best <u>*comforters*</u> in stressful times.

3. <u>Mental Triggers</u>
   - Negative <u>Thoughts</u> - Worry
   - Negative <u>Self-Image</u> – "I can't do this."
   - Critical <u>Self-Talk</u>. – *"What 's the matter with me?"*
   - <u>Forgetting</u> – When someone's mind is "overloaded," they start to forget important things.

<u>Identifying Stress Triggers</u>
Here are some questions to help analyze Stressful situations.
   - What are some examples of your Stress <u>Triggers</u>?

   - When Triggers happen, how high does your Stress Level go?

   - What do you see, hear and feel when Stressed?

STEP 3 - MODIFYING BELIEFS ABOUT STRESS

Challenging the Beliefs

The best way to overcome a stress trigger is to <u>write down</u> the "problem" and <u>challenge</u> it. Here is an example.

<u>Student:</u> I'm so stressed. I have 1,000,000 things to do.
<u>Dr. Perspective:</u> *Nobody* has 1,000,000 things to do. Let's make a list of the 1,000,000 things and see how many there *really* are. What's the first one?"

So, they write down the first one. Then, they write down the second and the third. By the time they get to 10, it is really getting hard. In a few minutes, they went from 1,000,000 "imaginary" things to about 6-10 *real* things. That alone should be a *load off* anybody's mind. "1,000,000 things" was a <u>False</u> and <u>Harmful</u> Belief to carry around, which was obvious once it was <u>written down</u>.

Common Stress-Inducing Beliefs
- *I'm so busy.*
- *I never have enough time.*
- *I have so many things to do.*
- *I am always late.*
- *I can't calm down.*
- *I am so tired.*
- *I always put things off to the last minute.*
- *I've always been like this.*
- *Nothing can be done to help me.*

<u>Running late</u> to meet someone is a stress trigger. The person might say things like, "*I am always late!*" Many people say things like that. Does it help? <u>NO</u>. It doesn't.

They are just <u>instructing</u> their subconscious mind <u>to be Late</u> by saying, "I am _always late_.". What if they said any of these other, more logical Affirmations instead,

- _I always plan ahead._
- _I am always on time._
- _I am smarter now._
- _I am going to learn from this._
- _Next time, I will be on time._
- _Next time, I will be 10 minutes early._
- _I can solve problems when I put my mind to it._

Worrying About the Bills?

Sometimes, even people with a lot of money have problems doing the bills. It's Boring, so they don't like to do it.

A Reactive Strategy is paying the bills when they are due. Sometimes, they remember, and sometimes, things get so busy, the bills get forgotten. That makes Life Harder.

A Proactive Strategy is to take all the bills as they come in and put them in a big envelope. Make a List of all the monthly bills on a sheet of paper in order of when they are due. Select a Designated Time (a specific _fixed_ time) like Saturday morning, Sunday night, etc. Review the bills then and pay the ones that are coming up soon. Finally, write down the date and amount that was paid on the List, so you can remember what you did. Put the rest of the bills back in the large envelope, and DON'T WORRY about them at all for the WHOLE WEEK.

That way, you don't have to worry about the bills except for only 20 minutes on 1 day a week. The rest of the week is not the time to worry about the bills. That can remove 1 stress trigger from your life.

Doesn't that make Life less stressful? If something comes to mind, just say, "*I will worry about that on Saturday morning.*" Of course, there might be an occasional *exception* for an <u>emergency</u>.

<u>Student</u>: Somebody would have to be very organized to do that. I am not that organized.

<u>Dr. Perspective</u>: Here are 2 options. Can you pick the one that is best for you?

- <u>Choice A</u> – Keep doing what you are doing and worry each day.
- <u>Choice B</u> – Spend 20 minutes each week paying the bills on <u>1 day</u>, and only worry about the bills only <u>once</u> a week.

STEP 4 – LEARNING RELAXATION TECHNIQUES

Most people know, when someone is upset and stressed out, the best thing to do is to "<u>*Relax*</u>." One successful Relaxation Technique is taking a <u>Deep Breath</u>.

RELAXATION EXERCISE: A Deep Breath

- Take a deep breath, and hold it.
- With your mouth closed, count backwards from 5 to 0. "*5, 4, 3, 2, 1, 0.*"
- Then, exhale. "*Aaaaaaaaaagh!*"

That can have very quick results because it puts more oxygen into the system. Some people do it twice.

Counting to 10?

An old "common sense" sayings is, "Count to 10." That sort of works, but it works better another way. Try counting <u>backwards</u> from <u>10 to 0</u>. Counting 1 to 10 is going "*up.*" Counting from 10 to 0 is going "*down.*" It is more relaxing.

Better yet, try counting backwards *very slowly* from 100 to 0. Some people suggest counting sheep to go to sleep. What if you counted sheep jumping over a fence in <u>*slow motion*</u> from 100 to 0?

You might actually do it the 1st time, but what will happen by the 2nd or 3rd time? Are you tired yet?

RELAXATION EXERCISE: Affirmations
Affirmations give instructions to the Subconscious Mind.
- *Relaaaaaaaaaaaxxxx.*
- *I can find my inner peace.*
- *I have the power within me.*
- *I can recall my Favorite Thoughts.*
- *It is such a pleasure to just Relax.*

Visualizing Your Treasure Chest of the Mind
Once someone learns how to relax by taking a deep breath and counting from 10 to 1, it opens the mind to many opportunities.

What if you recalled your Favorite Experiences from your Treasure Chest of the Mind (Ch. 3)? It is a way to easily change one's mental state. What if you did it for 5 minutes.

Wouldn't it be nice going to the beach, walking in nature, or seeing a beautiful view from a high mountain? Everybody can have a *Relaxing Place* in their mind. All they have to do is visit it *more often.* Since it doesn't cost any money, you can go anywhere you want. Hawaii? The Caribbean? A National Park? Paris or Rome? You can go anywhere you want at any time you want, and it's *free!*

The First Step
is
the Best Step.

STEP 5 - SETTING PRIORITIES

Learning a new job can be a very stressful experience. There are so many things to do, it can be a real struggle to get everything under control. A Daily Priority List can be a life-changer for working people, students, and parents.

Priority List

Day:_____   Date:_____

Write the Tasks and Time required for each Task.

1.

2.

3.

4.

5.

6.

7.

Do it now!

Tomorrow's Tasks

1.

2.

3.

4.

Lessons Learned

Suggestions for The Daily Priority List
  1. Do one sheet for each day.
  2. Start with writing down the Tasks to do in order of importance.
  3. If there are too many, put some on the Tomorrow list.
  4. Then, write an estimate of Time (2 hours, 10 minutes, etc.)
  5. When each task is completed, **cross it out**.
  6. Finally, write down any Lessons learned for the day.

When you write down the Time required for each task, you might find there are a few items that will only take 5 to 15 minutes or less. One strategy is to do those things first. That way there are fewer things to worry about. Instead of 7 things, there might be only 4 or 5 left. Each time you cross out a Task, you can see your progress and *feel better*.

This is a way to get "PLEASURE"
out of doing "Unpleasant" tasks.

Student: That's a lot of work. I could never do all that.
Dr. Perspective: Sure you could. Here are your choices.
  1. Ramble thought the day with no direction. At the end of the day, there are still be a number of uncompleted items. You might even complain about how you, "didn't get anything done and wasted the whole day."
     or
  2. Set a Daily Schedule with Goals and Priorities. Each time you cross off an item on the list, you know you have accomplished something. At the end of the day, you can get a Sense of Satisfaction because you are seeing all the accomplishments you crossed off.

STEP 6 – STRESS-REDUCING ACTIVITIES
Some activities can help reduce daily stress.
1. End Multitasking, which is trying to do numerous things at the

same time. Some people think it is "cool," but it doesn't work.
Instead, all that happens is a lot of things get done poorly,
and they take longer. Life can be more relaxed by just doing
one thing at a time.

2. Hobbies
    A Hobby can be a *counterbalance* to the high-intensity goal
    orientated parts of the day. Hobbies are valuable for
    reducing stress and enjoying a pleasant activity, which one
    gets satisfaction from and takes pride in (Ch. 15).

3. Exercise
    Most people have been told exercise is good for them. About
    25% of the population do not do any exercise at all. Just
    doing 20 minutes of exercise 5 times a week can have a
    significant impact upon a person's health and life span.
    Walking the dog can be a relaxing way to find peace of mind.

    Exercise revitalizes the body and reenergizes the muscles. It
    can also become a peaceful "private time" walking in the woods
    or a park. All the stress can be *left at the door* when you
    leave.

CHAPTER 10 - MOTIVATION

One of the most important elements of Happiness is being Motivated. Here is the difference.

- An <u>Unmotivated Person</u> can be Lost without any purpose. They can wander from one event to another. When faced with the smallest amount of adversity, they retreat back to their Comfort Zone.

- A <u>Motivated Person</u> has <u>Goals</u> they value and <u>Plans</u> directing the way toward achieving their Goals. There is great satisfaction in seeing one's progress toward a Goal each day (See <u>Chapter 14 - Goals</u>).

Basic Motivation

Motivation has both <u>Basic Principles</u>, which are rather easy to understand, and <u>Advanced Principles</u>, which can be a little more complicated.

<u>Basic Definitions:</u>
- <u>Dream</u> – A hazy vision about a pleasant thought in the future.
- <u>Goal</u> – A target. Something <u>specific</u> to shoot for that has <u>Numbers</u> and can be Measured.
- <u>Plan:</u> The path to the Goal, including numerous Steps.

- <u>Motivation</u> – An eagerness to achieve a Goal. It can be the reason someone works so hard to overcome adversity.
- <u>Adversity</u> – Something that is hard to do. An obstacle to achieving a goal.
- <u>Fear</u> – A feeling that something bad or dangerous is going to happen. A common reason for not trying.

Dreams and Goals

A <u>Dream</u> is an idea or vision. It is often hazy, without many details. A <u>Goal</u> is a Dream <u>converted</u> into <u>numbers</u>. That way, the Goal will have a numerical value to help <u>Measure</u> the Progress.

For example, suppose a charity wanted to raise $100,000 as a Goal. When $50,000 has been donated, they have completed 50% of the Goal. Numbers help the ability to "see" the progress, so it helps to create *enthusiasm*.

<u>THE PAIN VS. PLEASURE PRINCIPLE</u>

On the most <u>Basic Level</u>, people tend to,

<u>Flee</u> from <u>Pain</u>
and
<u>Move</u> toward <u>Pleasure</u>.

<u>The VERY BASIC Steps to Achieving Happiness (From p. 36)</u>
There are some specific things one can do to create happiness.
1. Define what Happiness is for you.
   Learn how to Recognize your Moods and Measure the intensity of your Emotions.
2. <u>Identify what Events, People, and Thoughts make you</u> **<u>Happy</u>**.
   - Do the things that make you Happy more often.
   - Learn how to *enhance* and *amplify* those things, so you can enjoy them more.
3. <u>Identify what Events, People, and Thoughts make you</u> **<u>Unhappy</u>**.
   - Do what makes you Unhappy <u>less</u> often.
   - Learn how to change the things that make you Unhappy to make them more enjoyable.

4. Learn how to <u>Switch</u> from Unhappy emotions to Happy emotions.

Of course, this is a very <u>oversimplified</u> analysis.

<u>The Problems with Pain and Pleasure</u>
<u>Student:</u> That sounds rather simple and makes sense.
<u>Dr. Perspective:</u> Here is where it gets complicated.

Can a <u>Painful Event</u> be seen as a *Good* Event and
a <u>Pleasurable Event</u> be seen as a *Bad* event?

Often, <u>"Painful"</u> Events can provide <u>Positive Benefits</u>.
It happens all the time.

<u>Student:</u> Now, I am really confused.
<u>Dr. Perspective:</u> The problems are:
- There are things people <u>like</u> to do, which are <u>bad</u> for them.
- There are also things people <u>don't like</u> to do, which are <u>good</u> for them.
- Overcoming Adversity (things people don't like to do) can provide the *Greatest Satisfactions* for Achievement.

A problem with the <u>Basic Pain and Pleasure Principle</u> is,

What feels "good" might
<u>not</u> always be "good" for us.

<u>Things that Feel "Good" but are Really Bad.</u>
- Being lazy and wasting day after day.
- Overeating can be unhealthy.
- Eating too much candy is bad for one's teeth.
- Spending an excessive amount of time watching TV or

71

playing computer games can take away from more social activities.
- Smoking, alcohol, and drugs are bad for one's health.

Things that are "Hard" and feel like "Pain" but are good.
- Studying hard in school.
- Working hard at a new career.
- Exercising to have a strong body.
- Eating healthy foods.
- Mastering Adversity.
- Doing the things you know you should be doing.

The LESSON is, sometimes,

We have to do the things we
don't want to do
in order to do the things
we want to do.

MOTIVATION FOR THE NEXT LEVELS
Abraham Maslow (1908-1970) was a psychologist who developed the Theory of Human Motivation. His idea was that there were various Levels of Motivation. The Physical Level, which includes the Pain and Pleasure Principle, is at the lowest level of motivation.

Read the Pyramid starting at the bottom - **1- Physical**.

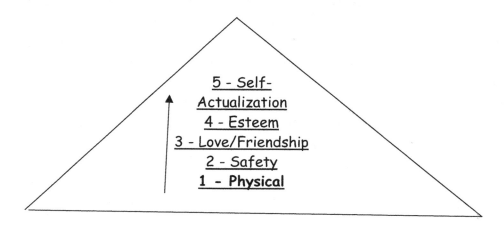

5 - Self-Actualization – Being creative. Achieving one's potential. Being what one can be.

4 – Esteem - Status and prestige. Recognition for personal accomplishments by others.

3 – Love/Friendship – Building relationships. Having friends and loved ones.

2 - Safety/Security – Being safe and secure.

1 - Physical – The immediate needs of the body. Food, water, and comfort. People flee from Pain and seek Pleasure.

Once a person achieves comfort for their basic needs in Level 1-Physical, they start seeking Level 2 - Safety and Security on a long-term basis. When those needs are achieved, the focus moves to Level 3 - Love and Friendship.

After that, achieving Level 4 - Esteem, including Status and Prestige, can take over in importance. Finally, when all those needs are met, the highest is Level 5 - Self-Actualization, meaning a person fulfills their creative accomplishments and their Potential.

By understanding the elements that motivate us, someone can start to do the <u>Activities</u> that move them up Maslow's hierarchy of needs. Not all people achieve the top levels.

In addition, it shows people can have many levels of Motivation <u>greater than</u> just physical Pain and Pleasure.

<u>DOING THE THINGS WE DON'T LIKE TO DO</u>

Everybody has activities they don't like to do. That's just normal. What if there was something one could do, so they wouldn't seem so "unpleasant?" There are actually many ways to do that.

<u>Managing Things You Don't Like to Do</u>
1. <u>Identify</u> the Things you <u>Don't Like</u> to do.
2. Determine why you <u>don't like</u> them?
3. Identify the <u>Benefits</u> of doing them.
4. Change the <u>Perspective</u> of the Event to find the "Good" in the "bad."
5. Change the <u>Event</u> from bad to Good, making it enjoyable.

Let's see if we can make some Difficult Tasks *less* painful and *more* enjoyable.

1. <u>IDENTIFY THE THINGS YOU DON'T LIKE TO DO.</u>
    Everybody has them. What are yours?
    -
    -
    -

2. <u>WHAT DON'T YOU LIKE ABOUT EACH TASK?</u>
    - Is it <u>too hard</u>?
    - Is it too easy, so you are <u>bored</u>?
    - Will it take <u>too long</u> to do?
    - Maybe, you <u>can't see</u> any reasons or <u>Benefits</u> for doing it.

There are solutions to those problems as we will see.

3. WHAT ARE THE **BENEFITS**?
    There are a lot of things in life we have to do that we don't like to do, but some of them are very necessary. Sometimes, they even provide valuable Rewards.

Student: How do I make any sense of all this?
Dr. Perspective: Often, when people don't want to do something, it is because they can <u>only</u> see the Pain.

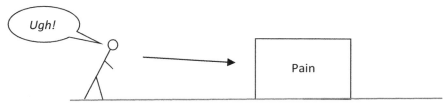

Motivation *starts* when they can "see" the <u>Benefits</u>.

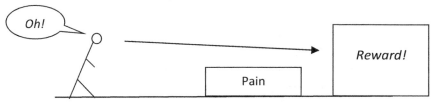

For example, suppose you were asked to do a dull, boring job for one hour. You might not want to do it. However, what if someone said they would pay $100 to do it. Would you be eager to do it then?

Student: Yea. Sure.
Dr. Perspective: That's because you are focusing on the Gain, instead of the Pain.

4 – CHANGE THE **PERSPECTIVE** OF THE EVENT

Another Perspective
A mother raising 3 children has a very hard and stressful life.

The kids are often screaming, making a mess, and getting into trouble (Pain). However, the mother is <u>Motivated</u> by an overwhelming <u>Love</u> of the children and the <u>Pride</u> of seeing them grow.

A Gym Perspective

There are other instances where advanced levels of motivation *override* the <u>Pain vs. Pleasure Principle</u>. Sometimes, weightlifters will use the expression,

"No Pain. No Gain!"

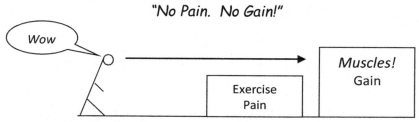

That is a use of <u>Perception Modification</u>, which looks *past* the Pain to *"see"* the <u>Gain</u>. Then, they are focused on the <u>Rewards</u>. The Pain is <u>not</u> seen as an Event in itself. It *is seen* as the <u>Path</u> to the Gain, which makes it a "good" thing.

Not Liking a Job

If someone dislikes their job, they will <u>not</u> be happier if they just quit the job. Without any source of income, they will be even more <u>un</u>happy. However, if they <u>choose</u> to get a <u>better job</u>, it might require getting more education or training. That could take some time to accomplish.

Instead of going to work each day thinking about how much they <u>don't like</u> their current job, they can start each day *focusing* on what it will be like to get their <u>Dream Job</u> soon.

Wisdom

In the middle of the Depression of the 1930s, a very difficult time, <u>Reinhold Niebuhr</u> (1892-1971) wrote the following strategy for coping with difficulties, which is popular today with some groups.

God, grant us the serenity to <u>accept</u> the things we cannot change,
the <u>courage</u> to change the things we can,
and the <u>wisdom</u> to know the difference.

This can be a great *stress reliever* because it separates those things that one <u>cannot</u> control from those things that can be changed.

If something is totally outside of one's control, the effort worrying about it is just wasting time. Instead, the effort can be *focused* on productive activities that can make a difference.

5 – CHANGE THE **EVENT**
What can be done to make Hard tasks less Painful and more Enjoyable?

Changing School
If a student doesn't like <u>school</u>, the solution is not to quit. If it is high school, that would make finding most good jobs very difficult. If a student is fortunate enough to be in college, dropping out would be something they will probably regret later in life. However, they could also <u>Change the Event</u> by selecting classes they are more interested in, changing to a better major, or transferring to another college they would like more.

Changing Pain into Fun
Doing <u>Exercise</u> is sometimes seen as hard and boring by many people. Coaches and trainers in the sports and exercise industry realized that. If everybody is bored, nobody will go to the gym and work out. The solution was to take exercise, something hard and boring, and make it more enjoyable.

Aerobics converts painful exercise into Fun by adding an instructor and music. The classes are 1 hour long. Just doing a whole class is a challenge, so the people who do it are proud of themselves. The high-powered music keeps everyone's mind energized. The instructor is a leader who *encourages* them to keep going. When it is over, everybody feels like they have accomplished something. They are healthier for the experience.

WAYS FOR MAKING UNPLEASANT TASKS MORE PLEASANT
1. Create a Competition
2. Use Music
3. Provide Rewards
4. Find Your Passion

1. COMPETITION - Creating a Competition is an old way to make something uninteresting very exciting. Since ancient times, games and competitions inspired athletes to compete for victory and praise. Today, companies sometimes have monthly and annual competitions that offer prizes and personal recognition. Schools offer awards to top students.

   If you don't have anyone to compete with, you can always compete with yourself. The secret is to write the event down and keep records. Suppose you have a task you don't like to do (sent out resumes to find a new job, pay the monthly bills, house chores, etc.). Just write down how long it took to do the task. That alone can provide a great incentive. Now, you realize there is an end to the task. Is it going to take 3 hours, 1 hour, or 15 minutes? The next time you do it, see if you can beat the "old record." You've just created a "Game" for yourself. Can you be a "winner" by beating your old time?

   If the task is going to take 60 minutes, you can keep track of the minutes to "see" your progress. That way, instead of focusing on how boring the job is, your mind is occupied with how to do it *faster*.

2. <u>MUSIC</u> - For boring tasks, adding <u>MUSIC</u> will make the time go by so much faster. That appears to be almost too easy. For thousands of years, there have been songs for:
   - Soldiers marching long distances
   - Sailors sailing on the oceans
   - Building the railroads
   - Harvesting crops
   - Inspiriting sports teams and their fans

Since they didn't have electricity years ago, they <u>sang</u> songs to keep their spirits up. Now, we have music to download or watch on Youtube.com. It is very simple but has worked very well for many centuries.

3 - <u>REWARDS</u> - Creating Rewards is something that motivates a person to get things done. When there is no reward, all someone will "see" is the "Work (Pain)," so why would they want to do it?

When <u>Rewards</u> are provided, they can *focus* on the Reward, while <u>overlooking</u> the Work (Pain). Often, just small rewards can bring big results.

<u>Using Pain and Gain</u>
Each day, many people have some things they <u>want to do</u> and other things they <u>don't want to do</u>.

What would happen if they used the things they <u>wanted to do</u> as <u>Rewards</u> to help them do the things they <u>don't want to do</u> (the unpleasant tasks)? A suggestion is,

always do the <u>Hard Thing first</u>.
That way you can have the
Fun Thing as a Reward.

Rewards can be simple like:
- A snack
- Listening to music
- Going for a walk
- Having a drink (soda, juice, coffee)
- Calling a friend
- Doing a Hobby
- Watching a favorite TV show

4 – PASSIONS
Some people work at jobs they dislike year after year. Another solution is to,

Find your Passion,
Something you *love* to do.

Then, see if there is a job you can do that has that activity. Life can be a lot more fun when you are doing something you like to do.

The Violinist
Lindsey Sterling loved to play the violin and dance hip-hop. Most solo violinists are in orchestras, and they don't like hip-hop music.

Despite the critics, she went to do what she loved with a Passion. After performing on America's Got Talent, she did some videos that became very popular. Then, she went on a world tour for 4 years doing what she loved.

One way to keep motivated is to just tell yourself,
"Good Job!"
when something goes really right.
That way you acknowledge your good effort.

CHAPTER 11 - PROCRASTINATION

Why Procrastination is so Stressful

Procrastination, by definition, is putting off the things one could do Now until "Tomorrow." Here are the Results.

- Continuously putting tasks off can cause numerous undone events constantly piling up.
- "Doing it Now" means you take care of tasks when they arise, so you don't have to *worry* about them anymore. The result is *less* things to do, *less* stress, fewer crisis situations, and more *time* to be Happy.

The reason why Procrastination is so counter-productive and stressful is, when a person puts an event off, the thought of the event "bounces around" in their mind until the task is done.

After a while, the pressure starts to build up creating a crisis. When it is done, it might end up being done in a panic, so the chance of it being done incorrectly becomes more probable.

EXERCISE: Creating a HABIT

A Procrastinator has a Habit. Each time they encounter something to be done, they say, "*I will do it later.*" They say it many times a day, and those undone events start competing for attention.

What if somebody used the same principle of a Habit to modify their behavior in a positive way.

Suppose somebody has a Task to do. Here are 2 strategies.

Strategy A – Put It Off

Instead of doing the task, a Procrastinator will put it off until "tomorrow." The next day, the person can have a 2nd Task to do, and they will try to put both Tasks off for the next day. On the third day, another Task arrives, so they now have 3 Tasks that should have been done. Their mind starts sending signals like, "You have 3 things you should have done, and they are not done. You are going to get into *trouble!*" However, the Procrastinator puts those 3 things off for the next day.

All that stress is <u>self-imposed</u>. There is really <u>no</u> real <u>purpose</u> for it. At some point, the person is going to have to <u>do</u> all 3 things anyway. The <u>Hard Way</u> is to keep putting them off until they become a last-minute *crisis.*

<u>Strategy B – "Do It Now!"</u>
The <u>Smart Way</u> would have been to just do the tasks when they appeared. That way they won't cause as much worry and stress. It is done today. That means it can be done without any pressure, so it can be done correctly.

<u>Steps to UNDO Procrastination</u>
1. First, realize Procrastination is a <u>Bad</u> and <u>Hard</u> way to live. It is the process of repeatedly putting things off, which means more stress and feeling uncomfortable. Too many times, waiting to the last minute offers the possibility of a mistake, which can mean it might have to be done a second time. Therefore, life becomes dominated by a <u>series</u> of daily Crisis Situations. Examples are:
    *   *"I am always late."*
    *   *"I forgot to..."*
    *   *"Why does this always happen to me?"*
    *   The car should have been serviced 3,000 miles ago.
    *   Students have to stay up late studying for a test, so tomorrow they will be too tired to do well.
    *   A birthday of a family member is forgotten.
    *   A letter didn't get mailed on time.
    *   You lost your keys and will be late again.

2. Create an Affirmation

The Procrastinator's Affirmation is, "I will do it later." They will say that many times a day to reinforce the Habit.

Here is a selection of Procrastination Affirmations, which can be much more productive.

- Do it NOW!
- Do it FIRST!
- Do it NOW, and you won't have to worry about it anymore.
- Don't leave it to the last minute. Do it NOW!"
- I will Do it FIRST, and enjoy the peace of mind.

Every time I say, "I will do it later."
I am creating stress.
Every time I say, "Do it NOW!"
I am reducing stress.

Just say the Affirmation numerous time a day. At first, it might not work. That is okay. Just keep saying it. Slowly, you might start doing a few things "now." Over time, the Subconscious Mind will start thinking, "You know, it really is easier to Do it NOW! It will only take a few minutes (or seconds), and then we won't have to worry about it anymore."

In time, it can become a Habit to, "Do it now!" That will make life so much easier.

LESSON: It wasn't the degree of difficulty that was holding the person back. It was the Habit.

Think it Through

This might be a very helpful process for self-motivation.

- If someone does the fun things first, they are already in a State of Pleasure, so why would they leave it to do something Hard/Painful?

- However, if they <u>always</u> did the <u>Hard Things First</u>, the Fun thing would be waiting as a <u>Reward</u>.
- When they do the <u>Hard Things First</u>, they want to do it very *<u>FAST</u>* because they want to get it over with, so they can do the <u>Fun/Pleasure</u> thing.

Either way, you have to do each task. The difference is one strategy creates worry, and the other creates satisfaction.

Every time you put it off,
The Habit gets weaker.

Every time you <u>Do It Now</u>,
The habit gets stronger.

There are numerous concepts in this book.
Just start by trying one you like at first.

1. People and Events can impact our emotions in seconds, but we can learn to use <u>pictures</u>, <u>words</u>, and <u>actions</u> to manage our emotions.
2. Happiness, like many other things, has a <u>Structure</u>, <u>Processes</u>, and <u>Techniques</u> that can be studied and mastered.
3. There are <u>7 Primary Tools</u> that can be used to manage Feelings.
    a. <u>Thoughts</u> can be used to create the desired Images.
    b. Modifying the <u>Self-Image</u> can be used to build Self-Confidence. The <u>Self-Image Exercise</u> brings our <u>Achievements</u>, <u>Skills</u>, and <u>Dreams</u> to our Conscious Mind.
    c. Many <u>Beliefs</u> are unproductive, but they can be replaced with powerful positive Beliefs.
    d. <u>Habits</u> are programmed in the Subconscious Mind, so they do activities without using the Conscious Mind.
    e. A <u>Negative Mental Attitude</u> looks for negative events, but a Positive Mental Attitude can be trained to look for the good events.
    f. The <u>3 Primary Sensory Channels</u> (Sight, Sound, and Action) can be used for learning and communications.
    g. <u>Mental Rehearsal</u> is a sports technology that has many applications for practicing social activities.
4. A Choice is whether we are going to have our Happiness determined by:
    *   Outside Events and People or
    *   Our own <u>Thoughts</u>, <u>Words</u>, and <u>Actions</u>.
5. Sometimes, there can be great pleasures discovered by just slowing down and enjoying "<u>The Moment</u>."
6. There are a variety of ways of interpreting Events including what one <u>Feels</u>, <u>Thinks</u>, <u>Says</u>, <u>Learns</u>, and <u>Does</u>.
7. <u>Stress</u> (Ch. 10) is the result of many activities competing

for the attention of the mind. Managing Stress can create a great improvement in someone's Mood. Each of the individual's Stress Triggers can usually be managed, but combined, they can cause health issues.

8. Identifying <u>Stress Triggers</u> makes it possible to reduce their impact. One of the quickest ways to manage stress is to just take a break and Relax. When we write problems down, they can be seen from a more distant Perspective. At times, just writing them down presents possible solutions.

9. Taking all the daily tasks and writing them on a <u>Priority List</u> is a way to identify the items that need to be done. Then, one can get the <u>satisfaction</u> of crossing each item off when it is completed.

10. <u>Stress-Reducing Activities</u> include ending Multitasking, doing Hobbies, and enjoying Exercise.

11. <u>Motivation</u> (Ch. 11) is one of the Keys to a Happy life. Having no motivation can be just wandering without purpose. Day after day can go by without getting much accomplished.

12. On the most basic level, Pain and Pleasure are the motivating factors. Pain can prevent people from trying, but it can also be a powerful motivator to recover from some bad event.

13. <u>Abraham Maslow</u> introduced the concept of a series of motivational levels after a person has satisfied their basic physical needs. So, there are numerous factors (Love/Friendship, Esteem/Prestige, and Self-Actualization) that are more powerful incentives.

14. Overcoming great adversities provides the greatest satisfaction.

15. There are lots of things people don't want to do, but with some creativity, they can <u>Change the Perspective</u> of the Event or <u>Change the Event</u> by using Competition, Music, Rewards, and Passion.

Student: That's a lot of information, but what can I do to be happier?
Dr. Perspective: Here are 5 answers to that question.

Happiness has a Structure. Like Abraham Maslow's Pyramid of Motivation, Happiness also has Steps or Levels of Satisfaction.

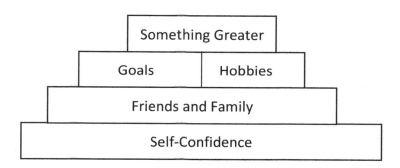

The Self-Image is the Foundation Block upon which everything else is built. The next layer is Friends and Family, which provides support and enjoyment for individuals.

At some point, they start to establish Goals, which provide satisfaction as they see Progress being made. When leisure time becomes available, Hobbies provide periods of relaxation to offset the intensity of achieving Goals. Therefore, Goals and Hobbies compliment each other.

At the top layer, many of the personal needs have been met. Then, a person can realize Life can offer Something Greater than just focusing on one's own personal pleasures. At that point, they start searching for something beyond themself.

Chapter 7 – The Primary Tools presented the concept of Self-Image using the Self-Image Exercise to identify personal Achievements, Skills, and Dreams.

BUILDING A POSITIVE SELF-IMAGE

How we "see" ourselves has a big impact upon how we "see" the world.

In sports, athletes practice their physical Skills, so they will get good at what they do. Their coaches also teach them how to Think in ways that build their Self-Confidence. However, most people don't practice the Life Skills of managing their thoughts and creating Happiness. Anybody who practiced daily to improve themself as much they practice their favorite sport would probably have a tremendous advantage in life.

Negative and Positive

Definition: Self-Image – How a person "sees" themself. These are the RESULTS of a negative or positive Self-Image.

Negative Self-Image	Positive Self-Image
Lacking in Self-Confidence	Having Self-Confidence
Staying in the Comfort Zone	Eager for challenges
Reluctant to meet new people	Comfortable in making friends
Unwilling to face adversity	Enjoying new experiences
Seeing themself weak	Seeing themself strong
Seeing the world as bad	Seeing the world as good

Building a Positive Self-Image is a Skill with a Structure and Processes, which can take some Practice over time.

Napoleon Hill (1883-1970) wrote the original Life Skills book, Think and Grow Rich (1937), which taught about using the power of the mind to achieve goals after doing over 20 years of research. His book contains 13 Principles, including how to create desire, overcome adversity, program the subconscious mind, and build one's Self-Confidence. His philosophy suggested imagining one's goals daily to overcome fear. His book is still a best seller to this day.

Clement Stone (1902-2002) dropped out of high school and started selling life insurance. That can be a very difficult business with a great deal of Rejection and hearing the word "No!" from potential customers. He struggled with Procrastination in his early years and overcome it by saying the self-motivator, "Do it NOW!" dozens of times a day. After achieving great success with his insurance company, he wrote Success Through a Positive Mental Attitude (1960) with Napoleon Hill. A major theme was building a Positive Mental Attitude as one of the Foundation Blocks of success and happiness.

Sports Psychology is a recent development in Olympic and professional sports. Before 1985, athletic training was 95% physical. Today, mental training is considered to be 50 to 90% of the reason a player or team wins a competition. Any team can have the talent, but it is Enthusiasm, Teamwork, and Desire that wins the games.

Dr. James Loehr (1941-2021) wrote the book Mentally Tough (1986), which identified 10 specific activities athletes can focus on and train to master. Some key concepts are attitude, motivation, visualization, psyching rituals, relaxation, and others to get into an Ideal Performance State.

The LESSON is, there has been a lot of research on how to help people perform better, be successful, and be happier. By understanding how our minds work and using Beliefs, Habits, and daily Practice, one can develop a Positive Self-Image in preparation for living a happy and productive life.

Many people go to the gym 3 to 5 times a week to exercise and be healthy. Others play tennis, basketball, soccer, or golf to keep fit.

What if, the same people dedicated an _equal amount_ of time toward _exercising_ the _mind daily_? Certainly, that would provide an improvement of their health and happiness. However, few do, despite the wonderful benefits.

What could the benefits be if someone spent just _5 minutes_ a day using the available tools like Visualization, Affirmations, and Journaling?

Here are the _ACTIVITIES_ that create a Negative and Positive _Self-Image_.

Negative Self Image	Positive Self-Image
Negative Self-Talk	Positive Self-Talk
Being Self-Critical	Encouraging oneself
Having Self-Pity	Finding the Blessings
Shying away from people	Building friendships
Flashbacks of negative events	Inspiring Dreams
Being Selfish	Being Generous
Focused on Self	Focusing on others

One way to measure a person's Self-Image is to listen to the vocabulary _Words_ they use.

Poor Self-Image	Strong Self-Image
Vulgarity	Enthusiastic words
Rude and angry words	Friendly words
Self-Critical words	Self-Empowering words

You probably know people who fall into both categories. Can you see how their words *influence* their Self-Image and their relationships with others? Another key to a person's Self-Image is the <u>Music</u> they listen to. Some music is angry and even violent in its content. Other music is cheerful, relaxing, happy, and inspiring. Can you imagine the impact that must make on them day after day?

To change your
Life,
change your
Thoughts.

After Self-Image comes <u>Friends and Family</u>, the second level. There are many components that create happy relationships.

For students, their ability to make friends will have a great influence on how much they enjoy school. In the work environment, making friends involves learning the skills of building <u>Rapport</u>, <u>Relationships</u>, and <u>Teams</u>.

<u>Definitions about making Work Friends</u>
- <u>Rapport</u> - Opening up a communication with another person. The process of getting to know someone *before* "getting down to business."
- <u>Relationship</u> - Once a Rapport is built, a "Relationship" or "Business Friendship" is created, so people can communicate together and help each other out.
- <u>Team</u> - A group of *people* with a common *Goal*. Ideally, a team has a <u>Leader</u> and a <u>Goal</u> the team members believe in. Skilled Teams Leaders are often promoted to high-level management positions.
- <u>Etiquette</u> - A <u>Set of Rules</u> for social communication. Different professions, companies, and countries have different rules of etiquette.

What is a Friend?
Friendships create a bonding relationship between 2 people which provides benefits for both parties. Friends often comfort and encourage each other in addition to enjoying each other's company.

Good friends are very valuable to have because <u>Friends</u> are one of the <u>Support Blocks</u> for happiness. Many people have never had any formal <u>instructions</u> on how to create and maintain friendships. It is something that is often learned by trial and error. It can be rather easy to learn once the basic principles have been presented.

Families
Families consist of parents, children, and grandparents. It is a relationship with traditions that go back thousands of years.

Love
One of the most powerful tools for changing mental states is Love. Someone can be sad and lonely one day. The next day, they might meet someone for the first time. Their life can change drastically. They can even go into a "state of bliss," which creates wonderfully happy feelings.

There are hundreds of helpful books available that focus on family issues and romantic relationships in great detail.

Friend - What Qualities Do You Look for in a Friend?
- What is a Friend?

- Why are friends important to you?

- What Qualities would an Ideal Best Friend have?

- What would they do for you?

- What would you do for them?

How Can You Make New Friends?

One idea is to take the list above of the things you want <u>from</u> a friend and do them <u>for</u> other people.

The Benefits of Friendships and Family

- Someone to talk with
- A partner to go places with
- Support in times of need
- Somebody to learn from
- Somebody to look up to
- Somebody to share with
- The status of being popular

<u>Basic Friendship Skills</u> – People without friends are often lonely, while people with many friends tend to be more enthusiastic. There are specific Skills for making friends.

- <u>Speaking</u> – The most basic skill is being able to speak to strangers. It requires the <u>Enthusiasm</u> to express oneself to others and the <u>Self-Image</u> to leave the Comfort Zone to meet new people.
- <u>Active Listening</u> - A key skill is <u>listening</u> to others. Most people talk too much (about themselves). Active listening is showing the other person you are <u>interested</u> in them by smiling, nodding, and asking questions.
- <u>Body Language</u> – The messages a person's body communicates can compliment or conflict with the words they say.
- <u>Asking Questions</u> – Asking questions is a way to gather information and show *interest* in others.
- <u>Teamwork</u> – When 2 people work together, they can create <u>Synergy</u>, which means 2 people can do more together than 2 working alone. It is sort of like…

$$1 + 1 = 3.$$

Four Important Qualities People Want From a Friend

1. Respect – Showing respect involves recognizing the other person as someone who is *important* and has *value*.

2. Empathy is when one person can imagine another person's thoughts and feelings. That might seem impossible, but with a little effort, most people can do it. Many children know how a brother or sister feels in response to certain events.

3. Support – A key factor in a friendly relationship is that each person supports the other. When one helps another, it builds the relationship and creates a stronger *bond*.

4. Generosity is offering time, friendship, and money to another person in need.

GETTING TO KNOW YOU

The First Impression can determine the success of a new relationship. If it goes well, the road will be smooth. If it is weak or awkward, it can bring a relationship to an end before it gets started. What determines a good first impression?

- A Smile and Eye Contact – These two are the "windows" of the mind and can offer friendship to others.
- Physical Appearance – Attire, posture, facial expression, neatness, etc.
- Body Language – What messages is the body projecting?
- Handshake – Is it lacking in confidence or feeling very comfortable?
- Voice Control – A strong and confident voice welcomes friends.

. An important LESSON is...

Body Language can speak
louder than words.

EXERCISE: Empathy – Can you determine the emotional state of another person? Seeing things from someone else's point of view is an important skill. How can you tell when a friend feels like this?

Happy	Relaxed	Mad
Sad	Confused	Scared
Lonely	Friendly	Withdrawn

What can you do to help them move from Negative Feelings to Positive Feelings?

EXERCISE: Asking Questions of a New Friend.
- "How are you?"
- "What's new?"
- "How is your day going?"
- "When did you join ____(the organization)____?"
- "Where do you live?"
- In a first business meeting, someone might ask, "What is your title?"
- "How long have you been with the company?"
- "Do you have a business card?"

EXERCISE: Making a New Friend – Imagine you are meeting someone for the first time. With a little practice, it can become natural.
1. Smile and make Eye Contact.
2. Introduce Yourself – "Hello." Shake hands. "My name is _____. What is your name?"
3. Give a Compliment –

4. Ask a Question –

Giving a <u>Compliment</u> is showing another person you are interested in being their friend. A <u>Question</u> is a way to encourage the other person to start talking. In Life Skills Classes, students often practice meeting people.

The First Meeting

A <u>first meeting</u> (or date) is an event where the <u>first impression</u> might set the tone for building a relationship. One person might be a little nervous. How can the other party make the nervous person feel more comfortable?

People in business have a lot of <u>first meetings</u> with customers, new employees, etc. Experienced business people are skilled at building <u>Rapport</u> and "<u>Reading People</u>." Is the other person for real? Are there any common interests? How could each party benefit from a relationship? Is the other person a "smooth talker," or can they be <u>trusted</u> to do what they say? Is this someone they want to spend more time with?

MAINTAINING FRIENDSHIPS

Friendships are also valuable to keep. The question is, what are some good ways to maintain and keep friends?

1. <u>Keep in Contact</u> – This can be done by visiting them, calling by phone, texting, and emailing. In addition, Social Media offers many options to keep in contact.
2. <u>Activities</u> – Parties, sporting events, concerts, and other social events are ways to strengthen friendships.
3. <u>Favors</u> – A <u>Favor</u> can be like an "invitation" or "gift" that offers Friendship. A drink or food can be a sign of saying "Welcome."
4. <u>Support</u> - This is one of the biggest friendship events and also one that is the most meaningful.
   - Helping someone when they are in need.
   - Pet sitting. Babysitting. House sitting.
   - Helping them move.

- Assisting when they are sick or injured.
- Being there in a time of crisis.
- Introducing them to other friends.

The more you put _into_ Friendships,
The more you tend to _receive_ from them.

Whether you _take_ from others, or
give to others,
They will likely _remember_.

Generosity and Good Deeds
Generosity and _good deeds_ do more than benefit the receiver.
They also _benefit_ the _Giver_ in many ways.

Forgiveness is another event that has _surprising_ benefits. What happens if a very bad event occurred many years ago? What happens to the person who is still angry and thinks about it year after year? Does that anger make them stronger or weaker?

What if the injured person _Forgave_ the one who did the bad deed and just forgot about it?

Student: That's not right. Why should somebody forgive a person who has done them wrong? What is the benefit of that?
Dr. Perspective: The person who did the bad deed can be far away and might have forgotten the event long ago. They might not even know when they are being forgiven. However, how does the Forgiver benefit?

They get released from the anger.

That would make for one less angry thought reoccurring in their mind creating more distress. Forgiveness can neutralize the negative memory and make it lose its power.

CHAPTER 14 – ACHIEVING GOALS

There are <u>Six Basic Steps of Goal Achievement</u>.

1. <u>Goal</u>
   Create a <u>Goal</u> and identify all the <u>Rewards</u> of the Goal.
2. <u>Plan</u>
   Develop a <u>Plan</u> with <u>Steps</u> as a *path* to the Goal.
3. <u>Desire</u>
   Use <u>Visualization</u> to imagine accomplishing the goal and enjoying the rewards. Use <u>Self-Talk</u> and <u>Affirmations</u> to increase enthusiasm on a day-to-day basis.
4. <u>Action</u>
   Take the <u>First Step</u> to learn how to do it.
5. <u>Record the Progress</u>
   Record the activities, so you can see the <u>Progress</u> and <u>Learn</u> valuable lessons from the experiences.
6. <u>Persistence</u>
   Keep going until the Goal is Achieved.

How Do They Do It?

Why do some people reach such high levels of success, when others just struggle trying to get by? Part of the answer is quite simple.

Many people are working at a "<u>job</u>" they don't like. If they lose their job, they might just "try" <u>something else</u>.

Exceptional Achievers are successful because they are pursuing something they <u>Love</u> to do. If something goes wrong with their job, they <u>try again</u> because that is what they want to do.

Hard Living vs. Fun Living

Hard Living is spending a lot of time doing what you don't want to do. When things go wrong, people give up and quit. Then, they try a new career doing something else. That means starting all over from the beginning in a new environment. They might start from the beginning a number of times in their life. Not only is that Hard, but they also don't get very far.

Someone enjoying Fun Living takes the time to find a job that is interesting to them. When they meet adversity, they Persist until they push through the adversity because that is what they want to keep doing.

There is a difference between...

Struggling with something you don't want to do, and
Doing something you love to do.
One is difficult, and the other is Fun.

Some of the things that make life Hard is using negative Self-Talk to say things to yourself like, "I can't." I'm not so smart." "I could never do that." A lot of energy gets wasted because people are often telling themselves negative and untrue beliefs.

Definition: Passion - When a person loves what they are doing. For some people, their work is their passion. That is part of being on Abraham Maslow's Self-Actualization Level, where they are making their dreams come true.

What is the HARD Way?
1. Having limited knowledge about life's Opportunities.
2. A limited Perspective (Me. Me. Me.) focusing on oneself.
3. Negative Beliefs.
4. Saying discouraging Self-Talk.
5. A negative Self-Image creates a lack of Self-Confidence.
6. Giving up at the first encounter with every adversity.

What is the FUN Way?

1. Continuously learning new knowledge that provides growth.
2. Focusing on other people helps make friends easier.
3. Replacing <u>false harmful</u> Beliefs with <u>true empowering</u> Beliefs.
4. Creating <u>Enthusiasm</u> with positive Self-Talk.
5. Building a Positive Self-Image with <u>Pictures</u>, <u>Affirmations</u>, and <u>Actions</u>.
6. Finding your <u>Passion</u> – Something you enjoy doing.
7. <u>Persisting</u> – Pushing on until your rewards come.

It's Too Hard!

When people take on a long and hard Task, it often appears so big, it is hard to imagine. The "Secret" is to <u>break it down</u> into many <u>smaller</u> Steps.

- The <u>First Step</u> is the hardest.
- With each Step, it becomes Easier because you are *learning* how to do it.
- By <u>Recording</u> your activities at each Step, you can <u>see</u> your Progress.

<u>Student:</u>   I don't like to have goals. All that happens is you don't achieve your goal, and then you are disappointed.

<u>Dr. Perspective:</u> As we mentioned before, there are great advantages to "<u>Living the Moment</u>." It can take ordinary events and make them extraordinary.

As often happens, what "feels good" can also become a negative event when taken to excess overtime.

There is a time to <u>Do</u> and a time to <u>Relax</u>. When each one is Managed and Balanced, things go fine. If one or the other takeover, it can be counterproductive.

One of the <u>greatest joys</u> in life are summer vacations while going to school. Students get out of school, and all they have to do is have fun all summer.

However, what happens when they get older? If they are overly focused on their own immediate pleasure, they risk waking up years later and asking themselves, "What happened?" The answer is, everybody else passed them by.

Time is valuable.
Someone can't get it back after
it was wasted.

Learning to Enjoy a Challenge

1. Can you find a way to convert the hard and boring Task into an enjoyable Competition? Often, you can compete against yourself.
2. Break large Projects into smaller parts.
3. Record events to see your progress.

As an example, let's imagine a five-mile race.
- A five-mile race is really five one-mile races.
- Runners time themself for each mile to recognize their progress.
- If the First Mile took 8 minutes, can they beat it during the 2nd mile?
- At 2 ½ miles, they are halfway there.
- At the 3rd mile, they have completed 60%.
- At the 4th mile, they can imagine the finish line is right up ahead.

This "Hard" Task can become Fun because Competition helps one...

see their Progress
numerous times along the way.

Can you apply those concepts to some tasks you are doing?

This is much better than being "Lost" and going in different directions not knowing when the event is going to end. The challenge is to take something <u>Hard</u> and convert it into something <u>Fun</u>, which makes you <u>want</u> to do it

Success is <u>not</u> just a Goal to be accomplished tomorrow.
Success <u>is</u> enjoying the Journey today.

The Secret is
to find your <u>Passion</u>,
something you love to do.

While a primary quality of being a Happy person is having a Goal one is interested in, it is <u>not</u> good to try to do it all day for 7 days a week. In fact, that would be very unproductive and unhealthy.

Work and commuting can easily take up 50 hours a week. Add in family obligations, and a person can have much of their time being very busy.

Some people work hard all day. Then, they crash in front of the TV exhausted.

A solution for offsetting the stress of the day's activities is to create a <u>Hobby</u>, which is a *counterbalance* to the high stress parts of the day. There are many popular Hobbies.

<u>Sports</u>

<u>Sports</u> can be enjoyed at various levels. The first is <u>playing</u> a sport. It is good exercise, and there is the excitement of winning.

In baseball, soccer, basketball, and football, there are many valuable <u>Lessons</u> learned in high school sports, Little League, etc.
1. <u>Mastering a Skill</u> through <u>practice</u>. Once someone does it the first time, it becomes easier.
2. Building muscles and burning fat makes one healthier.
3. Providing opportunities to learn the power of Teamwork.
4. One can <u>learn how to Lose</u> (accept failure), which is an important life lesson (<u>Ch. 19 - Learning from Failure</u>).

Another alternative is watching sports as a <u>Fan</u>. Image someone with a stressful job and many family responsibilities. The workweek can seem very long. On the weekend, they like to watch their favorite team play.

For the 2 or 3 hours of the game, they are involved in something very exciting. With each play, there is a chance to win or lose. Toward the end of the game, the excitement grows. Then, the final points are scored. The viewer might throw their hands in the air and yell, "We won!"

To some people, that's the highest score they achieved on the Happiest Meter for the whole week. That is why the price of tickets is so high. People will pay a lot for the sensations of having a winning experience. The tickets for the Super Bowl cost thousands of dollars, even though half the people will see their team Lose. That shows how much people LOVE to experience of winning.

Music
Music is another Hobby people enjoy because it changes their emotional states within seconds. Most people like to listen to music. There are many ways to download music, so it is easy to find the songs you love.

Others learn to sing or play an instrument as the next level. Learning to play the guitar or piano can take years to learn, but music can become a very enjoyable activity. It can also become a social event when they join a band or choir.

Exercise
Exercise is another enjoyable activity for many people. There is going to a gym, lifting weights, or doing aerobics. Many do it 5 times a week as a Habit.

The benefits include keeping the body fit, building muscles, and releasing all the body tension. Exercise is more pleasurable when someone keeps records. This is common with weightlifters, joggers, and bicyclists. How many miles can one do in a day, month, or year?

Swimming at the beach or pool is a wonderful relaxation activity in the summer. It can be even more fun with a friend.

Art also has various levels. Those who enjoy Art go to museums to see the paintings of famous artists. Then, there is creating your own drawings. It can take a lot of practice to be good, but it is fun being creative.

Games used to be board games like Monopoly or chess. Today, computer games are very popular.

Travel is a wonderful way to enjoy yourself. Many people remember Disney World as one of the greatest events of their life. Traveling to different countries can be expensive but memorable. Often, there are many interesting places to go right around where you live.

If you put the term "Things to do this weekend" into an Internet search engine, there will be lists of all kinds of things to do like museums, parks, festivals, shows, concerts, cultural events, historic events, celebrations, etc.

Reading is a way to travel in one's mind. Mysteries, romance, history, and adventure books become bestsellers.

Clubs
Clubs are a way to enjoy a hobby with others. There is Toast Masters, where people go to improve their public speaking skills. Social clubs provide many students and adults enjoyment because they can do events with new friends. There are golf clubs and tennis clubs. There are book clubs where readers discuss what they read and drama clubs that provide opportunities to put on plays.

Student: Okay. That is a lot of hobbies and clubs. So, what?
Dr. Perspective: That is a good question. Hobbies are beneficial because they *offset* the stressful parts of life.

In addition, clubs are a great way to meet new people and make more friends. If you join a team or club, you can instantly have the potential of meeting 10 or more new people.

Sometimes people think being happy is complicated. At times, it can be. At other times, it might just be asking yourself, "What would make me happy today?"

If someone is sad and lonely,
one of the best things to do is to
find Things of Interest
and Do them.

Warning: Of course, what you want to do can't be illegal, dangerous, unhealthy, dishonest, or mean to others.

CHAPTER 16 - SOMETHING GREATER

Most of this book has focused on the person. One of the greatest reasons people are <u>unhappy</u> is they spend too much time thinking about themselves. Every little "event" seems to be so *BIG*.

Two Philosophies

- <u>Philosophy A</u> - You are the most important thing in your life.
- <u>Philosophy B</u> - You believe in concepts (a purpose, cause, values, religion, helping others, etc.) beyond yourself.

In <u>Philosophy A</u>, the focus is totally about you. What were the important events of your day - School (a test), work (a project), what you ate for lunch, what mood you were in, a minor disagreement with someone, etc?

In <u>Philosophy B</u>, there may be "<u>Bigger Activities</u>" that can make those personal events, which are dominated by the <u>Pain and Pleasure</u> principle, look smaller.

Events that are Greater

Here are some concepts to consider.

- Kindness
- Generosity
- A Life Purpose
- Friends, Family, Children
- Religion
- Love

Looking from a Global Perspective

<u>Student:</u> I have so many problems. It is overwhelming. What can I do?

<u>Dr. Perspective:</u> That is rather simple.

Find someone who is worse off than you and help them out. Help

out at a homeless shelter. Go to the library and teach someone
to read. Sponsor a child in something they would enjoy.
Volunteer your time to a non-profit organization helping others.

When someone does things like that,
it can be surprising how many of
the "Problems" seem to go away.

People who are focused totally on themselves are easily impacted
by <u>minor annoyances</u>. However, when they have a <u>Vision</u> of
<u>Something Greater</u>, the little annoyances have less importance
and impact.

<u>Reality</u>
The reality is, if you are reading this book, you probably don't
realize how <u>Lucky</u> you are. Billions of people in the world have far
less than you. 3 billion people live on <u>less</u> than $2.50 a day. Many
never get a good education learning how to read and write
properly. Millions do not have clean water or enough to eat each
day. Imagine what life is like in Russia, China, or Iran, where
dictators run the countries and the people have no hope for a
better future. (Source: Globalissues.org)

You are one of the "lucky" ones.

<u>Student:</u> Me? I'm a lucky one?
<u>Dr. Perspective:</u> From a <u>Global Perspective</u>, many of your
"problems" might <u>not</u> be major problems at all. When you look at
the "Big Picture," instead of thinking about what you <u>don't</u> have,
you might start being <u>thankful</u> for all that you <u>do</u> have.

<u>From the Abraham Maslow Perspective</u>
Maslow's Theory of Motivation puts physical Pain and Pleasure at
the bottom of the Levels of Motivation. People are willing to
endure great hardships for causes they feel are more important.

Definitions:
   Fear – Real or imagine dangers in the future.
   Discouragement – When someone decides to give up.
   Hope – Wishing that something good will happen in the future.
   Faith – A belief in something positive which is beyond the available knowledge.

Some people can have their minds occupied by imagined Fears. Over time, they can become Discouraged.

Other people have Hope, an image of something good coming in the future. Faith is even stronger because it is a Belief not dependent upon facts or evidence.

Ending the Day Being Grateful
Counting one's Blessings is a valuable technique to end the day. What happened during the day? What can you be grateful for? A nice day? The company of a friend? A pleasant memory?

If someone writes the good events down at the end of each day, two things happen.
   1. The day ends with a Grateful Thought as they go to sleep.
   2. They can come back and recall their many Blessings numerous times in the future, especially when there is a "bad" day.

THE LAST OBSTACLES
THE SKILLS OF FEAR, ADVERSITY, AND FAILURE

There are 3 last <u>Obstacles</u> that can get in the way of Happiness - <u>Fear</u>, <u>Adversity</u>, and <u>Failure</u>

That means there are <u>3 Major Skills</u> available to overcome these obstacles:

1. The Skill of <u>Mastering Fear</u> – Chapter 17
2. The Skill of <u>Overcoming Adversity</u> – Chapter 18
3. The Skill of <u>Learning from Failure</u> – Chapter 19

There are different ways Fear can be seen.

The Perspectives of Fear
- Definition: Fear – A powerful emotion based upon visualizing future negative events that prevent people from moving forward in the face of danger.
- Alternative Definition: Fear - A *tool* that provides great energy activated by Adrenaline. When the powerful energy is focused on a goal, it can do amazing things.

The Comfort Zone

The Comfort Zone is a place in the Mind.

Outside   **Inside**   Outside

- Inside the Comfort Zone – Every day is the same. There are no worries, risks, or dangers. Everything is comfortable, easy, and peaceful. Nothing ever changes.
- Outside the Comfort Zone – There can be danger, discomfort, and risks. It takes a quick mind to survive and a lot of effort. However, there are great *opportunities* for excitement, growth, and rewards.

When people become aware of these two options, some want to stay Inside their Comfort Zone. Others get restless inside and want to go Outside to see what Opportunities will present themselves.

Can the Fear Become Greater than the Event?

Sometimes, students in a Life Skills class learning How to Find a Job are reluctant to come up in front of the class and make a presentation.

112

There are 2 options available:
- Go to the job interview without practicing their presentation and make it up in front of the interviewer.
- Practice their presentation in front of a friendly teacher and other students to work out the "bugs" and build Self-Confidence.

The reason for the reluctance can be <u>Fear</u>. However, what is there to be afraid of? The teacher is supportive, and the other students are friendly.

So, what is the problem? Will the classroom "practice event" have any physical danger? No.

Is it more likely their mind <u>flashed</u> back to some past Negative event, possibly a far back as childhood. Did somebody laugh or make fun of them a long time ago?

When other students go before them, they realized it might not be so bad.

As they finally decide to "try it," they might be nervous at first. After they complete their presentation, they often become very happy as the rest of the class cheers and applauds them for their effort.

People can conquer their fears by doing the things they were afraid to do when they go <u>slowly</u>. The <u>LESSON</u> is, their <u>Fear</u> of the Event was <u>far greater</u> than anything that could happen to them in the friendly classroom environment.

By taking <u>small steps</u> to conquer their fears, they finally...

enjoyed the <u>excitement</u>
as their Self-Confidence soared.

That does <u>not</u> mean anyone should take any big physical risks or do anything dangerous. Instead, by taking <u>small</u> steps one at a time, their confidence can grow with each small success.

<u>Napoleon Hill</u>, in his book <u>Think and Grow Rich</u> included a chapter entitled, "*The Six Ghosts of Fear*," It presented how to identify and overcome fear.

<u>There are a variety of common fears.</u>
1. The <u>Fear of Failure</u> is one of the most common types of fear because people don't like to be disappointed.

2. The <u>Fear of Criticism</u> means a person is afraid that others will say bad things about them. It can be very powerful. To prevent that, people often choose to <u>not</u> try doing what they want.

   The question then becomes, <u>who</u> is the person who is making the critical remarks? Is it...
   ▪ A parent, teacher, or responsible person offering good constructive advice?
   ▪ A good friend who is trying to help?
   ▪ Someone who has a different point of view?
   ▪ Someone who has a lot of anger and likes to criticize and bully other people?

   There can be constructive comments that are valuable and helpful. There are also mean and angry people, who just want to criticize others and make them also feel bad.

   People who have high goals often have <u>critics</u> who are jealous and envious. What does an angry person dislike the most?

   A Happy Person

When a critic has such unhappiness and anger within themself, they want everyone else to be angry with them. A Bully is typically someone lacking Self-Confidence. That is why they always pick on someone weaker or younger than they are.

People who are happy with themselves are usually *nice* to others. In fact, they can even help others out when they need support. That makes them *more* friends who respect them for their kindness.

3. The Fear of Rejection results from one person offering friendship to another person and having their offer rejected, which feels like they are being rejected. What if others frown, laugh, or even mock them? Typically, that is something many people want to avoid because it is outside their Comfort Zone.

   The reality is, many times, what we want to achieve requires "social risks" to achieve our happiness. An example might be when someone starts trying to meet new people or get a new job. It would be nice if, the first time they met someone they became best friends. It would be wonderful if, on the first job interview, everybody got a great job. However, that rarely happens.

Here are the options:
1. Avoid any future attempts to meet new people,
   or
2. Try again knowing it usually takes many attempts to find a new best friend or an ideal job.

This can be hard to do whether someone is young or older. That is because they can:

- <u>Focus on the Pain</u>, and try to avoid it
  <u>or</u>
- See <u>beyond</u> the Pain and <u>Focus</u> on the <u>Rewards</u> to get what they want.

<u>EXERCISE</u>: <u>Smile Competition</u>
If someone feels uncomfortable in social situations, they can <u>practice</u> being friendly by smiling and saying hello to the people they meet each day. It might be some people will not smile back, but it is a great way to learn to master the Fear of Rejection.

What if, you tried to make a large number of people smile each day. All it would take would be to smile and say something nice like, *"Hello!" "How are you today?"* What if you had a contest with yourself to see how many people you could make smile in one day?

The first day might be hard, but the First Step is always the hardest. Soon, it becomes much easier.

How many people could you make smile in a week? Pretty soon, <u>they</u> would <u>start smiling</u> as soon as they saw you coming.

Wouldn't that help build your Self-Confidence?

Emotions vs. Logic

The <u>Right Brain</u> is dominated by <u>Emotions</u>. The <u>Left Brain</u> is dominated by <u>Logic</u>. Often people are presented with a conflict between <u>how they feel</u> and what Benefits them.
- I'm really angry and don't feel like doing it (Emotions), <u>but</u>
- I know trying again is the best way to achieve my Goals. (Logic).

This can be a hard topic to understand. It might even take some time to learn it in the real world.

The Big Lesson is:

Many people have never been taught the Skill of Mastering Fear, so...

> Their emotions dominate their actions.
> That means they have little control.
>
> Once they think through their options,
> they have the opportunity to choose
> the Perspective (Emotions or Logic)
> that is best for them.

Solutions to Fear, Worry, and Stress

The first solution to Fear is to just Relax. This can be done by taking a deep breath and using Visualization Skills to imagine a relaxing experience.

EXERCISE: Visualizing Relaxation to Create Peace of Mind

- Shut your eyes and take a few deep breaths.
- Imagine (See) a peaceful Image (picture) like a walk in the woods on a beautiful spring day.
- Say some relaxing words – "I can find my inner peace."
- Take Action – Can you imagine petting a friendly dog or cat? How would a big hug from a good friend make you feel? What if you tried to do something you have been putting off for a long time? You can do these things in your imagination or reality.

EXERCISE: Writing a Letter

Another old technique is to write a letter expressing your fears and anger. Then, save the letter for the next day. When you are more relaxed, read the letter. Then, throw it away. Another option is to save all the letters in a private place. A month or year later, you can read and reflect on the letters from the distance of time.

Do you think your opinion of the event would change over time? If you looked at some letters after a year, would you be laughing at how silly they seem? Fear of failure, criticism, and rejection can be difficult things to overcome. However, when they can be analyzed from different Perspectives, they can become easier to master one step at a time.

CHAPTER 18 – THE SKILL OF OVERCOMING ADVERSITY

There are 2 concepts about Adversity that are helpful to understand:

Life is <u>Hard</u>,
and
Life is <u>not Fair</u>.

However, when you understand that,
it actually becomes much easier.

<u>Student:</u> What? Why would you tell me Life is hard and unfair? That just makes things worse!

<u>Dr. Perspective:</u> No. It will actually make things much *better*. When students are young, their parents take care of them and protect them. As they grow and leave the nest, many are not really prepared for what is ahead.

The *reality* is, Life can be <u>Hard</u>.
There will be many Adversities over time.

Also, Life will <u>always</u> be <u>unfair</u>.

Somebody is always going to have more, and somebody always is going to have less.

<u>Student:</u> No! No! No! That's all wrong. It can't be that way!

<u>Dr. Perspective:</u> If someone thinks life will be Easy and Fair, who will they blame when they run into their first real adversity? Many things that happen are <u>outside</u> our control. Sometimes, people blame themselves when things go wrong, even when it's <u>not</u> their fault.

When they encounter something that is "unfair," they might stop and say, "Oh. That is so unfair. I don't want to do it anymore."

That strategy will <u>not</u> be successful.

<u>Two Life Perspectives</u>
- <u>Person A</u> thinks life will be easy, so they never prepared for it. When they meet their first adversity, they might withdraw and give up. *"How could this happen to <u>me</u>?"* *"What did <u>I</u> do to deserve this?"* What will that solve?
- <u>Person B</u> realizes Life can be Hard and Unfair at times. They *expect* challenges and are <u>not crushed</u> by a little setback or an encounter with something that is "unfair." Instead, they think, *"When I <u>overcome</u> this challenge, I will be <u>stronger</u>."*

If a person believes <u>Option A – Life is Easy</u>, what happens when things they want don't come easily? Who will they blame? The probability is they will blame themselves.

"Why can't <u>I</u> do this?
What is wrong with <u>me</u>?
<u>I</u> *can't do anything right."*

That can be the fast road to <u>Self-Pity</u>.

If someone is really going to be Happy, they have to <u>accept</u> that occasionally there is going to be "rainy days." Otherwise, the "rainy days" will dominate over the pleasant events.

If a person can accept <u>Option B – Life is Hard</u>, then, the problems are <u>not</u> the result of <u>unrealistic expectations</u>. The problems are from the <u>outside</u> and are often <u>not</u> their "fault." When they look at life more realistically, hopefully, they will <u>not</u> be so self-critical.

Student: That still doesn't make any sense to me.

Dr. Perspective: It can be a difficult concept to understand at first. However, when something goes wrong <u>later in life</u>, you might be able to <u>look back</u> and appreciate what this means.

In fact, it is more likely that you won't appreciate this Lesson for <u>5 or even 10 years</u>. When a major event happens, you can think back and realize how to use this information then.

<u>Definitions</u>

Adversity can also be viewed in different ways.

- <u>Definition: Adversity</u> - A hardship or difficulty. Something that is hard to do.
- <u>An Alternative Definition: Adversity</u> – A task that is hard, so it makes people stronger.

Student: How does that concept help anyone have a <u>Positive Mental Attitude</u>?

Dr. Perspective: At first, this might seem to be just the opposite of what you would want to hear, but there are great Benefits.

<u>Three Advantages of Adversity.</u>

- <u>Benefit A – Adversity Creates Strength</u> - The harder the Task, the stronger the person gets.

- <u>Benefit B – Adversity creates Wisdom</u> – The more adversities that occur, the *more lessons* a person learns.

  <u>Wisdom</u> is the Knowledge built up after years of learning Life lessons from trying *many* things.

- <u>Benefit C – Adversity creates Opportunities</u> – Since many people seek to avoid adversity, it creates great <u>opportunities</u> for those who are willing to push *forward* and *overcome* difficult tasks. As someone overcomes one adversity after another, they grow <u>stronger</u> and become <u>wiser</u>. As a result, it builds their Self-Confidence which opens up new opportunities they never imagined.

<u>Another Perspective</u>

<u>Malcolm X</u> (1925-1965) grew up in a very bad environment. However, he later said,

> *There is no better than adversity.*
> *Every defeat, every heartbreak, and loss*
> *contains its own lesson on how to*
> *improve your performance next time.*

<u>Student:</u> What? How can something "bad" be good?
<u>Dr. Perspective:</u> Learning how to <u>overcome</u> events that are <u>hard</u> can take a <u>long</u> time. However, one can start to learn new concepts like:

- <u>Persistence</u> – The Skill of not giving up but *pushing on* until the goal is achieved.
- <u>Resolve</u> – The idea that, *"When the going gets tough, the tough get going."* When difficulties arise, the <u>longer</u> they take and harder they are, the <u>more determined</u> a person can become.

Imagine how much stronger someone becomes just understanding that "Persistence" and "Resolve" are real Tools. Many people never heard of the concepts.

The adversity makes them become <u>mentally</u> tougher and <u>physically</u> stronger, so they are able to handle future adversities.

Big rewards are often provided BECAUSE things are Hard. If everything was easy, everybody would be doing it. When things are Hard and take a very long time, many people will never even try. Others will give up very quickly. That will create many valuable Opportunities for the very few people who Persist to receive the rewards.

<u>Student:</u> Are you sure?
<u>Dr. Perspective:</u> Yes. The only way to grow and gain wisdom is to take on *many* hard tasks. That way you become <u>prepared</u> for and <u>willing to accept</u> failures as the *necessary* <u>Steps</u> to the Rewards.

Suppose there are 2 people.
- <u>Person A</u> never got out of the Comfort Zone and never tried anything hard.
- <u>Person B</u> took on many hard tasks and learned the value of "Persistence" and "Resolve."

Who will be better equipped to master Life's problems – Person A or Person B?

A common example is going to college, which takes 4 years of hard work. The people who achieve it have much better job opportunities because of the knowledge they learn during the 4 years. A master's degree takes an additional 2 years of specialization in a specific skill. So, that *extra effort* provides them with the knowledge and skills to get <u>even better</u> jobs.

A Story About the Canoe Trip
<u>Milton Erickson</u> (1901-1980) was a psychiatrist who change many of the ways we solve difficult social problems. During his time, he was so far above everyone else, all the others could do was Model (copy) him.

What made Milton Erickson such a genius? Was it natural talent? Probably not. It was said he had a problem with <u>dyslexia</u> as a youth, so he had a vision problem that made reading difficult. He was also tone-deaf and color blind for the most part. In addition, he got polio at the age of 17 and used crutches or a wheelchair most of his life. None of these things would suggest he had any extra "talent" or advantages over others.

Possibly, the reason why Erickson was such a genius was because he _had_ to work at life _harder_ than everyone else. In fact, he was quoted as saying, polio had given him an "_advantage_."

The rest of the people could read easily, but he had a _reading disorder_ (dyslexia). Most people can walk, but he had to _teach himself_ to walk again when he was recovering from polio. Some people play football to keep in shape. Erickson could _not walk_ without crutches, so football was out.

Someone once told him he should not exert himself physically because of his polio.

Instead, he decided to go on a 1,200-mile canoe trip one summer by himself to _build up his Self-Reliance_. Since he took very little money, he had to live off the land. So, he _chose_ an extremely difficult task to overcome his physical disabilities.

Dr. Perspective: So, what do you think about the _Benefits of Adversity_ now?
Student: I still don't get it.
Dr. Perspective: Try this. There were 2 runners.
  - _Runner A_ ran 2 miles a day 3 days a week.
  - _Runner B_ ran 5 miles a day 5 days a week.
Which runner will be in better shape at the end of the summer?
Student: Well, I guess the runner who ran the 5 miles.

Dr. Perspective: There were 2 students.
  - _Student A_ studied for 1 hour a night.
  - _Student B_ studied for 3 hours a night.

Which Student will get better grades?

Student: The student that studied for 3 hours will get the better grades. Everybody knows that.

Dr. Perspective: Are you starting to "see" the Benefits of Adversity? It is a Path toward building strength. People learn many valuable lessons from adversity.

Student: Do you mean, when I learn all these things, everything is going to go right for me, and I won't have any problems?
Dr. Perspective: A baseball team can practice their skills until they are very good. Are they going to win every game they play?
Student: No. Even the best teams don't win every time.
Dr. Perspective: Correct. After someone learns their skills, it is not a guarantee the rest of their life will be perfect. Instead, it means they can be happier than they were before. One reason is they will be able to learn from the events that don't go their way.
Student: Okay. Okay. I get it now.

Summary of Mastering Adversity
- The harder the Task, the more you learn.
- The harder the Task, the stronger you become.
- The longer it takes, the more experiences you have.
- The more experiences you have, the Wiser you become.
- The greater the challenges, the greater the rewards.
- The more frustrated you get, the prouder you feel when it is finished.
- It teaches people they can do more than they thought they could.
- Without adversity, they would never know what their potential is.

CHAPTER 19 – THE SKILL OF LEARNING FROM FAILURE

Napoleon Hill, In <u>Think and Grow Rich</u> (1937), wrote,

"Every adversity brings with it
the Seeds of an Equivalent Benefit."

Hill lived during the Great Depression of the 1930s and World War II. He wrote a book entitled <u>You Can Work Your Own Miracles</u> (1972). It was not exactly a book about how to be rich in 30 days. Instead, he wrote about the 20 greatest "failures" of his life. Some took years to overcome.

<u>The Seeds of Equivalent Benefit</u> means, in every Adversity and setback,
there are <u>opportunities</u> to learn powerful lessons,
if someone looks for them.

The <u>Benefits of the Failure</u> can often be
<u>GREATER</u> than the loss from the original "Event."

In other words, Negative Events do not have to be seen as "failures" using the <u>Perspective of Time</u>. Instead, Hill's <u>Lesson</u> was, each setback provided him the knowledge and strength to conquer the next adversity. Hill's belief was, it takes a <u>Positive Mental Attitude</u> to be able to "see" the <u>Benefits of Failure</u>.

- <u>Failure</u> teaches lessons.

- The <u>Pain</u> provides the <u>motivation</u> to think, "*What will it take to end this pain?*"

- <u>Failures</u> can become "<u>accelerated learning experiences</u>" that provided the <u>directions</u> for the achievement of success in the future.

- "Failures" make us aware of what does <u>not</u> work, so we can focus on better things that will work.

- Things that partially work provide the path toward the Goal.

"Failure" can be seen in many ways, which totally depends upon one's Perspective.
- <u>Definition: Failure</u> – When something goes wrong and does not succeed. A disappointment. Something discouraging. <u>or</u>
- <u>Alternative Definition: Failures</u> – <u>Required Steps</u> to achieving Goals. Often, it takes many <u>Learning Experiences</u> to be successful.

An Event can be seen as a...

<u>"Failure"</u> making it a "disappointment,"
or
a "<u>Learning Experience</u>,"
which provides new solutions,

<u>A Baby's Learning Process</u>
A baby is a <u>learning machine</u> trying different sound combinations until they say words, which might take a year to accomplish. They are also continuously <u>inspecting</u> the various objects they find to determine what they do and how they can be used. Nobody taught the baby how to do it. It just happened naturally.

<u>Success in Baseball is a Result of Perspective</u>
If a batter has a batting average of <u>.300</u>, that would mean, for every 10 at-bats, they <u>failed</u> 7 times. Someone who does not understand baseball would think the batter was a failure, but players and fans see them as a *STAR!*

A Super Star's Perspective

"I've missed more than 9,000 shots and
lost 300 games in my basketball career.
In 26 games, I was trusted to take the
game-winning shot and missed.
I've failed over and over in my life,
and that is why I succeeded."

Basketball Star Michael Jordan

Michael Jordon's quote suggests:

Option A – Avoiding failure and never trying will <u>not</u> work.
<u>but</u>
Option B – Failing many times <u>increases</u> our chances of
<u>winning</u>.

A Hockey Perspective
You miss every shot you never take.

Hockey Star Wayne Gretzky

In other words, if you never try, you will never win. The quote
also suggests "<u>not trying</u>" can be seen as "failing."

Teaching the Skill of Losing
Coaches have to <u>teach</u> players <u>The Skill of Losing</u>, so they don't
become be self-critical and give up. They specifically teach
athletes to,

Put the loss <u>behind them</u>, and
Focus on the <u>next</u> game.

If a player keeps thinking about the "Loss," they will carry the
bad emotions into the next game. Then, they will lose <u>2 games</u>
because of 1 event.

The Worst?

There was a construction manager in charge of a number of large projects. At the weekly meetings, it was common for the different subcontractors to bring up various problems. Sometimes, the meetings got a little intense because a lot of money was involved. After everybody argued for a while, the manager would often say,

"What's the Worst?"

What is the <u>worst thing</u> that could happen, and what will it <u>cost</u>? Oddly enough, that would actually *calm* things down. Many times, the actual amount of money was quite *small*. Asking, *"What's the worst?"* often puts things into <u>Perspective</u>. Determining the price of "The Worst" can make the problem appear <u>smaller</u> because...

The fear of the <u>unknown</u> was replaced
by a known <u>dollar</u> amount.

When someone identifies the "worst" in terms of dollars, it can put a "<u>limit</u>" on their fears.

The Playoffs

Most sports have the Playoffs at the end of the season. EVERY TEAM <u>loses</u> their <u>last</u> game, except one (the Champion).

When the next season starts, the players are expected to come to training camp with a *whole new attitude.*

<u>The Skill of Losing</u> is a valuable Skill to learn
because
Losing is far more common than winning.

So, there should be <u>no</u> shame in it.

<u>Falling Off a Horse</u>
There is an old story about falling off a horse.

When you fall off a horse,
get right back on.

If you sit around thinking about the fall, all you do is *magnify* it in your mind.

The longer that memory lingers, the *harder* it can be to get back on the horse. That is because you are thinking about the fear and can start to lose your Self-Confidence by constantly reimagining the failure. So, waiting a day or week may make it *more difficult* because it gives the negative memories time to grow.

However,

If you get <u>right back on</u>,
your last memory is <u>not</u>
the image of falling off, but the
<u>Pride</u> of <u>getting back up</u>.

<u>Failing</u> is a <u>Skill</u>
that can be taught and learned.

SUMMARY - CHAPTERS 12 - 19

1. There are 5 Building Blocks upon which Happiness is Built.
2. The Foundation Block is Self-Image.
   - The way someone "sees" themselves has a significant impact on how they "see" other events and people.
   - Sports psychologist Dr. James Loehr identified 10 mental concepts (attitude, visualization, affirmations, etc.) that can be mastered one at a time.
   - Many of those concepts can be applied to non-sports activities like personal development and being happy.
3. Friends and Family provide valuable support for individuals. In work environments, building relationships and teams are advanced skills that companies seek in management positions. Learning the vocabulary and etiquette can require significant effort when joining a new organization.
4. Achieving Goals has specific Steps for planning, motivation, and taking action, which can lead to increased performance. Making "Hard" tasks fun makes achievement easier.
5. Hobbies provide an alternative to the intense activities of goal achievement.
6. After one has satisfied their personal goals, many people find they want Something Greater than just the satisfaction of their own physical needs. That is when the great rewards come.
7. Traditional Fear, Adversity, and Failure are obstacles that prevent people from achieving their Dreams and Happiness. However, each Obstacle can provide many hidden Benefits.

While numerous techniques have been provided, the major concepts are also important.

1. <u>The Biggest Concept is</u>,

<u>HAPPINESS is a Skill</u>

...<u>instead</u> of something controlled by heredity, one's childhood environment, daily <u>Events</u>, or other <u>People</u>. It is not some mystery with people searching for the "magic secret." While all of those elements do have an impact, the ability of a person to <u>Learn</u> can overcome all of them with practice.

The <u>Role Models</u> provide examples of people who overcame very severe personal issues but had very productive lives.

<u>Anne Sullivan</u> was abandoned as a young child and then became blind. What possible hope could there be for her, yet she earned her place in history for giving love and guidance to Heller Keller, who was worse off than she was.

Most people think running a Marathon (26 miles) is a superhuman task only a very few ever try. Why would anyone even dream of running 31 marathons in a row? Yet, <u>Rob Jones</u> did it to prove to himself and other veterans that his disability would <u>not</u> define him. Instead, by performing such an *unimaginable* event, he became an inspiration for so many others.

Some people know <u>Thomas Edison</u> was deaf and had limited public schooling. Most assume it was because of his hearing. In fact, he was sent home from school with a note from his teacher that he was "unteachable" after 3 months. Much later, at the age of 12, he got scarlet fever which caused his poor hearing.

Therefore, he had 2 major disasters in his life which would have victimized most other people.

After being criticized for "failing" to invent the lightbulb after 10,000 attempts, he used the lesson of Persistence to change the world after he finally succeeded. He later said,

> I never did a day's work in my life.
> It was all fun.

Despite his major disadvantages, his days were full of *excitement* and *joy*.

Milton Erickson, the famous psychiatrist, had a reading problem (dyslexia), so he read a dictionary numerous times because the family did not own many books. He was both tone-deaf and color blind. Instead of being held down by the weakness of his senses, he became the *innovator* in the use of multiple senses in communication and learning, who promoted the applications of the Primary Sensory Channels.

One time, he spent over 1,000 hours helping one client. By applying that much effort frequently, he discovered many quicker techniques to improve the lives of others.

To compensate for his inability to walk without crutches, he spent the summer paddling a canoe over 1,200 miles and living off the land to build his self-reliance. What other student would even think of spending their summer vacation all alone doing that?

It seemed he concentrated on his weaknesses until he became a master of them.

It is doubtful that many readers of this book have hardships similar to those Role Models. The <u>LESSON</u> is, they overcame things most people could not imagine to enjoy productive and successful lives.

2. Each generation <u>does not have to start from scratch</u> learning the "common sense" information that makes up Life Skills. There is plenty of *existing information* available to learn from.

3. Once someone can see the <u>Structure</u>, <u>Processes</u>, and <u>Tools</u> for being happier, they can <u>choose</u> from the tools available, depending upon their interests.

4. <u>Fear</u>, <u>Adversity</u>, and <u>Failure</u>, which are often perceived as great obstacles, can create Skills that provide wonderful benefits.

It doesn't mean someone has to be extraordinarily strong, amazingly determined, and willing to sacrifice all pleasure to achieve some huge goal.

Instead, it is better to just pick one or two techniques and give them a try for a start. Some are really easy like <u>The Smile Competition</u>, <u>3 Good Things about Me</u>, and <u>Making a New Friend</u>.

Remember,

The <u>First Try</u> is the hardest.
However, it is also the one you learn the <u>most</u> from.
After that, things get easier.

5. The best way to <u>Learn</u> something is to <u>Teach</u> it. That is why so many people receive so much joy from teaching others how to reach more of their potential. A good way to start is to offer them the Affirmation,

"I can learn to
be
Happier."

Think of all the people who are frustrated, discouraged, and lost without any guidance. How much could YOU accomplish with just a little effort and some kindness to help family and friends find their hidden Potential?

Just start small and try 1 or 2 techniques. What if you started with just 5 minutes a day to practice? It might be using Visualization to improve your dream, the Treasure Chest of the Mind to recall your memories, or Mental Rehearsal to practice your skills.

Can you imagine the JOY of teaching others how to have:
- Self-Confidence and try new things
- Strong Friends and Family relations
- The ability to achieve Goals
- Interests in new Hobbies
- The knowledge that there is Something Greater that is so powerful, it makes all the little problems go away?

Remember,

Happiness
Is
Contagious.

Other Amazon.com publications by Jerry Dykstra in this <u>6-Book Life Skills Series</u> include:

The Book of Life Skills – 52 Life-Changing Lessons
Affirmations – Words for Self-Confidence
How to Make Friends – A Guide to Social Skills
How be Smarter – The Skills of Learning-to-Learn
Happiness is a Skills – Techniques to be Happier
Visualization – Techniques for Imagination (late 2022)

Knowledge is Power.

Education is the key to a better Life.

If you can understand and apply just some of these concepts, the impact could be…

Life-Altering.

For more information, or to write a review, go to:

Amazon.com > Books > Jerry Dykstra

If you enjoyed the book, it would be very helpful if you could write a <u>review</u>. That way other people can enjoy it.